Bennett Books
Sherborne House Editions

At Sherborne House in the village of Sherborne in Gloucester-shire, England, an extraordinary experiment in passing on tech-niques for spiritual transformation took place from 1971 to 1976. This experiment, the International Academy for Con-tinuous Education ("Sherborne"), was based on the method of a *fourth way*, a term attributed to G.I. Gurdjieff that describes a psychological and physical environment for accelerating the pro-cesses of spiritual transformation. Under the personal direction of J.G. Bennett, more than five hundred adults and children from around the world gathered for five yearlong residential intensives. It was at Sherborne that Bennett lived until his death in December 1974; and it was during these years that his lectures and writings most intimately addressed the needs of a coming new age of spiritual perception.

Bennett Books Sherborne House Editions presents material given out by J.G. Bennett during these years. This material is timely and wholly relevant to the 1990s—a time during which the present barriers between the worlds of spirit and matter will become even less apparent and the barriers between people will further diminish.

Other Sherborne House Editions:
> *Sacred Influences: Spiritual Action in Human Life.* 1989.

This *Sherborne House Edition* is printed on 60 lb. acid-free paper.

About the Cover

The Ark

Sacred tradition records examples of the relationship of the spiritual to the material world for the "building" of a "ship" in times of change. Here are some examples.

Ancient Indian: *The ship of Manu*

"Manu, however, was to be preserved by the help of the Fish, who commanded him build a ship and go on board with the seven Rishis, and with the seeds of all existing things."   —*Maha-Bharata, The deluge story.*

Sumerian: *The ship of Ea*

Tear down this house, build a ship!
Give up possessions, and seek thou life!
Despise property and keep the soul alive!
Aboard the ship take thou the seed of living things.
    —*The Epic of Gilgamesh, God [Ea] instructing Utnapishtim.*

Hebraic: *Noah's Ark*

"And of every living thing of all flesh, two of every *sort* shalt thou bring into the ark, to keep *them* alive with thee; they shall be male and female."
    —*Genesis 6.19, God [Yahweh] instructing Moses.*

We have chosen for our cover illustration *Noah's Ark,* a late thirteenth century miniature, because we wish to bring attention to a service worthy of a New Age community: the construction of an "ark" in which the good is preserved for future generations. We gratefully thank the Trustees of the British Museum for this privilege.

Needs of a New Age Community

J.G. Bennett, 1974
The day before he died.

Needs of a New Age Community

Talks on Spiritual Community and Fourth Way Schools

J.G. Bennett

(Compiled and edited from talks given to his students during the last three years of his life. Except for chapter 2 and part 1 of chapter 6, which were given in 1968.)

With a foreword by Mrs. A.L. Staveley

Bennett Books
Santa Fe, New Mexico

Originally published in 1977 by Coombe Springs Press
New material has been added

BENNETT BOOKS
P.O. Box 1553
Santa Fe, New Mexico 87504

© 1990 The Estate of J.G. Bennett
All Rights Reserved
Printed in the United States of America
96 95 94 93 92 91 90   5 4 3 2 1
First Bennett Books Edition 1990

Cover art: Noah's Ark. Miniature in North-French style. Hebrew MS.
Late 13th century. © 1976 The Trustees of the British Museum.

Book design: AM Services
Frontispiece photo by Avis Rappoport Licht
   © 1990 by the photographer

Library of Congress Cataloging-in-Publication Data

Bennett, John G. (John Godolphin), 1897-1974.
   Needs of a new age community : talks on spiritual community and
fourth way schools / J.G. Bennett ; with a foreword by Mrs. A.L.
Staveley. -- 1st Bennett Books ed.
         p.   cm.
   "Compiled and edited from talks given to his students during the
last three years of his life, except for chapter 2 and part 1 of
chapter 6, which were given in 1968."
   Includes bibliographical references.
   ISBN 0-9621901-2-8 : $11.00
   1. Spiritual life.   2. Sermon on the mount. I. Title.
   BL624.B396   1990
133--dc20   89-18562
                                                                CIP

The present work contains material not appearing in the original
Coombe Springs Press edition. The appendixes, publisher's notes,
biographical note, and bibliography of J.G. Bennett have been added
to this edition.

Contents

✧

Other books by J.G. Bennett

REFLECTIONS OF THE REAL WORLD

BENNETT BOOKS dedicates this publication to all those who, in searching for the "real world of human existence," try and fail and try and fail and dare to try again. Their persistence spites only their failings; they continue and endure—thereby making for themselves a "raft that leads to the far shore."

Bennett Books publishes material that reflects the work of those who have crossed the "waters of difficulty." Their lives are evidence that transformation is possible and, indeed, our human right and obligation.

—The Publisher

COME, COME, whoever you are,
Wanderer, worshiper, lover of leaving—
it does not matter.
Ours is not a caravan of despair.
Come, even if you have broken your vow
a hundred times.
Come, come again, come.

—Jelal-ud Din Rumi

Foreword

IF YOU HAVE NEVER READ THIS BOOK BEFORE, I recommend that you begin with the chapter in the middle, "The World Situation," and then go back to the beginning and work your way to the end. Even if you have read the book previously, it is still good to begin with that chapter.* The picture that Bennett paints was ahead of its time, but we can now confirm the accuracy of his vision. He indicates a direction to be followed. If any of us—members of humanity at large—are to make our way through the difficulties, present and to come, then almost certainly this is the direction to be followed. Mankind must learn and practice how to work together, how to serve instead of exploiting one another. More importantly, we need to realize and acknowledge that man as he is—man as we are—is helplessly adrift. There is no way to extricate ourselves on the level where we exist. We are obliged to look where we have accustomed ourselves not to look, to a level higher than ourselves, for the direction to go in order to save not only ourselves but even the very planet we live on. And there is no more time to waste.

The situation has accelerated since this book was written. Everywhere there are those who, as Bennett says, are dimly aware that at this moment in time there is a spiritualizing influence in our

*"The World Situation" is now the first chapter of this revised edition.

1

world and that this action comes, as Gurdjieff puts it, "from Above." How can we respond to and cooperate with this force, become its instruments? He also reminds us that "the spirit cannot work without the flesh," which is another way of saying what the Lord's Prayer tells us in the form of a petition:

> Thy kingdom come. Thy will be done
> in earth as *it is* in heaven.

This presupposes that some of us will be able first to know and then to practice the Will of the Father. Many people today in many places hear a call toward this end, but as it is also true that "many are called and few are chosen," how can we take that step that will enable us not only to follow the call but also to choose ourselves as effective instruments for actualizing the task? Community: it's one thing to theorize about it and another to work toward bringing it into being. Where are the companions? Where is the guide?

It becomes increasingly clear in large-scale as well as small-scale matters that the foundation, the core, of all that is askew in humanity at this present time is the relationships we have with one another, whether it be man with man or nation with nation. Everywhere there is suspicion, fear, hatred, violence, though at the same time there is no lack of voices calling for trust, understanding, love, forbearingness in our mutual relations. Obviously, ears to hear these voices are needed and, after that, real endeavors to learn how, actually, to change first our attitudes and values—that is, what we feel is important—and afterward the way we live. It is noteworthy that there are many efforts being made at this time by people on all parts of the planet toward forming small communities founded on one idea or another. A template is required, and this cannot be found on the level of ordinary life. Consequently, most of these attempts are doomed to failure. To find the template requires (1) a special form of intelligence that recognizes that help from a level higher than the one on which we exist is needed and (2) a willingness on our part to give up many of the notions and values cemented into us by our lives or, if you prefer, by society.

Bennett says a good deal about the Beatitudes in this book. These are practical advice meant for those who, two thousand years ago, seriously intended to try to actualize here on this earth principles and laws from a higher level. These are, if practiced, an indispensable help toward the only end and aim worthy of man as he could be, and they are as applicable now as they were when first compiled. It is as clear now as it was then that a community of those with similar aims is a necessary basis. For one thing, to practice loving God by beginning with neighbors requires accessible neighbors with the same aim! However, two thousand years have passed, and not only is the situation of man infinitely more precarious than it was at the time when the Roman Empire fell but the whole world, the whole planet, is affected. More is needed. Humanity itself is starting from a different place from where it was at that time. Although it is obvious that there is a wide current of destruction flowing through mankind in general at this time, there are signs that the attempts to learn to work and live together are also here as evidence of something new beginning. The direction is clear everywhere: small groups of people grope to find a way to work together; to live together; to have less wasteful, less abnormal lives; to turn the current of alienation, separateness, egotism to something more becoming.

Those who make a study of Gurdjieff's book *All and Everything,* or *Beelzebub's Tales to His Grandson,* find that it provides what is most needed in a very practical way. It belongs to this age. Of course, just as with the Beatitudes, it is addressed to the deepest part of us—a part with which we have almost lost touch—the part where man's conscience lies buried. But any community of people wishing to find the way to prepare for the "kingdom of heaven" here on our earth will need to find again the guiding conscience in each one, that impulse in us that, though inaccessible at present, is still our real potential. Gurdjieff died in 1949 but said himself that he put all he knew into his book.

This book of Mr. Bennett's, which you are about to read, really underlines the need for the practical aspect of a teaching, whether that of Jesus or of Mr. Gurdjieff. The New Age community struggling to raise itself in a vertical line—off the horizontal preoccupation with how to make their ordinary lives more agreeable and with materialistic ideas of what a community's needs are—will find much help in Bennett's as well as Gurdjieff's book, though that cannot come about instantly. It takes work and study, but for those who persevere, what amounts almost to a blueprint for living and working together begins to appear—not, as one might suppose, in the books but in the people who study them.

To understand completely, however, many are needed who are willing to listen to each other. Listening in this way is one of the first needs in working toward an effective community in a practical way—once one has accepted the fact that help from a higher level is required in order that the laws and principles of that higher level can be more nearly actualized here.

It is hoped that *Needs of a New Age Community,* this very foreseeing book of Mr. Bennett's, will have a wide circulation.

—Mrs. A.L. Staveley
Two Rivers Farm, Oregon
October 1989

✧

A.L. STAVELEY lived in England for more than thirty years, and it was there that she met Jane Heap, with whom she studied the ideas of Gurdjieff. In 1946, at the end of the Second World War, she and her fellow pupils traveled to Paris to study under Mr. Gurdjieff himself. They continued traveling there to study with him until his death in 1949.

Mrs. Staveley lives in rural Oregon at present. There, together with a few other people, she studies Gurdjieff's ideas by experimentally putting them into practice—that is, by actualizing on a farm what has been understood.

Foreword
[to the original edition]

FOURTH WAY SCHOOLS on the lines of the International Academy for Continuous Education were to be the preliminary step in setting up communities that would live in a way corresponding to the needs of the future. Tens of thousands of experimental communities have been tried in recent years, and most have been found wanting. The Sherborne experiment has shown that high levels of cooperation and discipline are possible but not how they are to be maintained without artificial conditions and technical leadership. It is therefore more than theoretical interest that is bound up in publishing the talks Mr. Bennett gave on the requirements for New Age communities. But there is no formula in these talks. A formula would have to be imposed and regulated in operation by some kind of oligarchy or elite, and this would destroy the balance of the society and produce regression to a hierarchical structure. How is it possible to have in a community genuine self-sacrifice and love that is not imaginary? The answer is in a combination of know-how about the production of energies required for our cosmic role and understanding the evolutionary potential of the "denying principle." Only those who have become awakened to the world of energies and are prepared to struggle with denial inwardly instead of outwardly can form the new kind of social order. But they must also find an outer task; they cannot withdraw into isolation.

These talks include Mr. Bennett's commentaries on the Sermon on the Mount. He regarded the sermon as a *legominism* based on the enneagram, transmitting special knowledge to the future as well as being a record of how people were able to realize the revelation of love and live through the terrible times at the beginning of the first millennium after Christ. The final notes [chapter 7] have been compiled from fragments written down almost verbatim after an unrecorded talk. They are intended to convey the flavor of the undertaking of a new way of life.

—A.G.E. Blake
Sherborne House, England
October 1976

✧

A.G.E. BLAKE was a student of J.G. Bennett's and assisted him at Sherborne House. He compiled the original edition of this work. Blake presently lives with his wife and six children in Gloucestershire, England.

WE ARE NOW too close to each other for the old kind of individualism to be bearable: the interaction is too powerful. What is in front of us is the need to change to an attitude in which we accept that every man has to serve a cosmic purpose, that every life serves for something, not just for its own satisfaction and not for some otherworldly purpose either.

Chapter 1

The World Situation

IT IS HIGHLY IMPROBABLE that the world will get through the next thirty years without some very dramatic events, particularly events that have to do with the working of our society. Our society is not adapted to withstand the strains that will come; it can cope only with changes that are slow. It is based on complex institutions such as those that deal with the production and distribution of goods. The institutions have very large bodies and very small brains, like the dinosaurs that are now long extinct. They work from a primitive instinct of self preservation according to traditional patterns of behavior and response. They do not work even with the intelligence of an individual human being. When the inevitable shortage of necessities comes about, they will not be able to adapt.[1]

There are many people who have already lost confidence in institutions and the way of life they now dominate. Their first reaction has been to put all their attention on what is wrong—all the stupidity and destructiveness—and we had that period of the 1960s, the period of political activism. People tried to stop the development of destructive weapons, to stop wars, to promote social justice, and to combat racism. This ended in a very wide disillusionment. People saw, without understanding it, that something worked to make things become their own opposite. They saw that the people who tried to work for peace played into the hands of those who created war; that those who tried to liberalize institutions played into the hands of the hard-liners; and that those who worked for decentralization provided weapons for those who wanted to concentrate military or industrial power in the hands of the few, whether management or labor or of whatever political ideology.

Now, in the 1970s, there is already a different climate. People are tending to look for a way of life that ignores or even discards institutions. There are two important trends that are apparent in heavily industrialized areas such as Japan, Europe, and North America: one is

7

the tendency to group together in small communities, so that now there are tens of thousands all over the world; the other is to look for quick ways of transformation, of arriving at a new kind of life independent of the outer-world forces (there are large-scale spiritual movements that many millions of people are experimenting with).

In my view, there will be a general disillusionment with all of this by the 1980s. That will be the time of the onset of panic. Visible loss of trust in the institutions could come about explosively if there were a sudden shortage of foodstuffs, and just a few years of bad harvest would be enough. But even without that there will be panics. This does not mean a time of revolution and sudden collapse. Governments and institutions will try to adapt to the changing climate of thought and feeling in the world. It will then become evident that things cannot last as they have been and that what is needed is a change in attitude that today very few are able to accept: a change from the tendency (of the last two or three thousand years) to regard expansion as a good in itself to a different life attitude that even regards contractional concentration as a good in itself.

Such a change of attitude is so much against things as they are now that it will truly be a revolution. Every one of us, in spite of what we think, remains geared, for all practical progress, to expansion and the belief that we are living in a climate of expansion. There are very few of us who are really prepared to look for a way of life in which we would live with less instead of more. The lesson cannot be learned by common sense because people close their minds to it. It can be learned only by bitter experience. That bitter experience will come in the period of time from the 1980s to the early part of the next century. By then, either we shall have got through, or we will have collapsed.

This period is the greatest opportunity that has existed for many thousands of years for "the Work." Not for thousands of years has there been such a need for people who are able "to work." The reason for this is that the transition from one system to another can come only through the "third force."[2] It cannot come from the passive majority or the active minority, from the governed or the power possessors.

If we talk of the role of the Work, we must understand that this is not the usual perspective. Everyone, in some way or other, recognizes that we are in a moment of great transition, but for the most part the predictions made by people are entirely humanistic. People look at the human situation and what man can achieve. By and large, they ignore the defects of human nature and take it that man will behave fairly, if not very rationally, and will make use of his intelligence and creative powers to build a world in which the achievements of man's intelligence will play a dominating role. The picture is of man increasing his domination over the material world and of achieving mastery even over forces that at present are too strong for him, such as the forces of disease and old age, to create a future that is secure for the human race. There is no regard for the consequences to the natural order, and there is no attempt to answer, or even ask, the questions "What is it all for? What really will have been achieved by all this?"

There are optimistic and pessimistic predictions. The optimists look at the accelerated rate of change and see the world in a hundred years' time as far more changed from ours as ours is from that of a hundred or even a thousand years ago. The pessimists look at the consequences of unlimited growth and seriously question whether it is possible for mankind to survive, it being impossible to restrain our thirst for more. Neither the optimistic nor the pessimistic predictions take into account the working of higher forces or the presence of some higher purpose. We, however, try to take into account forces that are higher than man and largely incomprehensible to us. We look at this time of transition as something not due just to the action of human agencies but to the working of higher forces and higher laws.

We need to understand the role of these higher influences. Gurdjieff, in presenting the right life for man, put among the "five obligolnian strivings"[3] that man should strive to know ever more and more about the laws of world creation and world maintenance. This striving is put on the same level as paying for our existence, striving for the perfection of our being, helping our fellowmen, and fulfilling our obligation toward the Creator.

One of the consequences of that enhanced power to learn about nature, which man has gained in the last hundred or so years, is that we have pushed back the boundaries of our knowledge not only out into space but also backward in time. We have a totally different historical perspective. We can see the history of man over a million years and even discern some of the details.

The evidence tells us that there is a law of accelerated evolution. This means that changes now take place in a human lifetime that have never before happened in the history of the Earth. The evidence also tells us that there are cycles in human life. These are the "epochs" where a master idea that is compelling an attitude toward human life pervades the world.[4]

The climate of thought of the last epoch has been based on the sacredness of every human life and the right of every human being to his own fulfillment. This has worked itself out and brought us to a point of saturation in the desire for more, to fulfill oneself by being more even at the expense of others or at the expense of nature.

We are now too close to each other for the old kind of individualism to be bearable: the interaction is too powerful. What is in front of us is the need to change to an attitude in which we accept that every man has to serve a cosmic purpose, that every life serves for something, not just for its own satisfaction and not for some otherworldly purpose either.

Gurdjieff started with the question "What is the sense and significance of life on the earth and in particular of human life?" Our lives are not our own. Gurdjieff says, "Why do you take such care of your sheep and cows? Is it because you want their lives to be happy and successful, or is it because you want their meat and wool and hides? Don't you see that it may be the same with you? Why shouldn't there be some superhuman farmer who feeds you and takes care of you because he needs something from you?"

When I first heard this idea, I was shattered. I could not reject it as absurd. I had always been sure that we must exist to serve some purpose. The mutton and wool doctrine means that the higher powers are not so much interested in our lives as in our deaths. A sheep becomes a salable asset when it has been slaughtered. Gurdjieff even went so far as to suggest that wars occur on the earth when more human deaths are required.

Our lives must serve some better purpose than the satisfaction of our personal desires and ambitions. The idea that the aim of life is "the pursuit of happiness" has got the world into its present trouble. But this does not mean that human life on the earth need be as meaningless and frustrating as most lives are today.

Man is not merely a domestic animal serving the needs of the higher powers. He has a very high destiny, but he can attain it only if he earns it. Hitherto this destiny has been expressed in terms of reward and punishment: the "goodies" go to heaven and the "baddies" go to hell. This no longer makes sense, for we know very well that everyone is mixed up: no one is good enough for eternal bliss, and no one is bad enough for eternal damnation. It is absolutely necessary to find a totally new way of looking at human destiny if we are to make sense of our lives.

We see round us suffering and injustice. Virtue is not rewarded, wickedness is not punished. We see mankind helplessly drifting toward a wretched state of overpopulation, depletion of resources, and wholesale pollution of our Mother Earth. There is a real danger of total disaster by way of an atomic war. A new horror is on the horizon in the shape of new diseases to plants, animals, and man. An era of fresh plagues that chemotherapy will be powerless to cure has been predicted. Altogether, prospects for the next fifty years are pretty terrifying.

Can these horrors be averted? Shortly before he died, Gurdjieff predicted the troubles and also the way to prevent them.

The "wool and mutton" that man is required to produce is not his own flesh and blood, but energy. There are psychic energies as well as physical energies. All that we experience—thoughts, feelings, sensations, joys, and sufferings—are forms of energy. People do not know about energies, and so they fail to produce what they might and waste most of what they do produce.

Gurdjieff showed us how to produce psychic energies of the kind required by nature and also those needed for our own self-perfecting. Everything that lives produces energies, and all forms of life need one another.

One of the axioms of ecology is that all life is one. Every form of life—vegetable, animal, and human—depends on other forms of life to supply the energy it needs. We men and women, too, have to provide energy for higher forms of life.[5]

We can do this blindly—automatically and helplessly—by living and dying with no regard for our obligations toward the planet that is our mother. Or we can consciously, by our own efforts, work to increase and store these precious energies. In doing this, we not only fulfill our duty toward the Earth and the Moon, but we create for ourselves our own souls.

True happiness is the aim of all life; however happiness is not achieved by pursuing it. Real happiness is spontaneous and comes when one is living according to one's nature. The trouble is that few people know their own nature or what real happiness is.

Real happiness comes from the secure feeling that one is doing the right thing in the right way. People crave security and do not see that there is no security unless one is doing the right thing.

So Gurdjieff says that we must first know ourselves, that is, our own nature and its potential. Our nature requires energy. We must produce that energy by the way we live our lives. Gurdjieff taught us the secrets of energy production and conservation. There are not only physical energies like heat, gravitation, electricity, and cohesion; there are also psychic energies of thought, feeling, organic sensation, and sex. These energies can be concentrated and blended by means of special exercises and meditations. They can be released in activities needed by ourselves and others. They can also be donated by us to that cosmic purpose that Gurdjieff calls "feeding the moon."

We can know this Earth intimately and the Solar System very sketchily. The rest of the universe is known only from afar. On this Earth we can see the appearance and evolution of life. Evolution does not go by itself. It is an apparent violation of the Second Law of Thermodynamics that tells us that all that exists must degenerate. Evolution needs energy, and it needs just the kind of energy that we people alone can produce. This is our obligation toward the Earth and the Solar System. At certain moments when a big step forward is to be made, a great concentration of energy is required. It happened when man appeared just before the Ice Ages began, and it happened again when modern man appeared thirty to forty thousand years ago.

The energy needed is released when a living being dies, but it can also be produced by our own efforts. The second way also gives us something for ourselves. That something is a higher form of being that can be called a "soul."

Gurdjieff insisted that no child is born with a ready-made soul but with only the potential for acquiring a soul. Those who do not acquire their own soul perish, as Gurdjieff always expressed it, "like dirty dogs."

A man with a soul is happy, for he has a perpetual sense of security; nothing can touch or harm him. There is no more exciting or satisfying ambition than to acquire one's own soul and help others to do so, too.

The old world is past saving. During this present century the first great disaster has already occurred. This was due to the failure of mankind to recognize the enormous responsibility we incurred through our great technical discoveries, especially the release of energy through steam and internal combustion engines and electrical generators. This release of energy threw the world out of balance. Only conscious people could have rectified it. According to Gurdjieff, there was a group in Tibet who could have saved the world.[6] But their leader was killed by a stray bullet when the British invaded Tibet in 1902, and the rest of the group died soon after. This group knew the secret of generating the spiritual energies needed to neutralize the destructive forces released by our technical discoveries. Gurdjieff had learned a part of this secret and passed it on to us. It is the answer to his question "What is the sense and significance of human life on this earth?"

Because of the disaster in 1902, the world collapsed. Two world wars and the loss of forty million lives were the visible consequences. The breakdown of human societies and the threat of a third world war were before us in 1950, but strange things happened that averted the final tragedy.

Now we must think of saving the New World. We continue to make technical discoveries and release more and more energy. If we succeed in harnessing the energy of atomic fusion, a really frightful situation will arise. The work started in Tibet a hundred years ago will have to be resumed on a far greater scale.

To save the world, three different kinds of action are required: one is visible and two are invisible. The visible work is to prepare the new social order. We shall need "work communities" or, as Gurdjieff called them, "Fourth Way schools." These will be devoted to training people to survive and develop under the severe conditions of the next hundred years. These schools will have the practical task of creating self-supporting communities able to work together and share resources and also to help their environment. This is much harder than it looks.

Modern man is a taker and not a giver. Whoever has power uses it to take and hold, whereas the only right use of power is to give and share with others. It is possible to go far enough in the elimination of egoistic grasping after one's own benefit to be able to live and work in a community. But this requires teaching and training. That is what Fourth Way schools are for, but only on the exoteric, or outer, plane.

The deeper, mesoteric, work is concerned with energies. Psychic and spiritual energies must be released, concentrated, stored up, and put to work in the right way. This requires very special knowledge and readiness to work and sacrifice. There are schools in the world that are doing this today, but they are not in the West. We need to take up this work ourselves.

If people are willing to undertake such work, they must first be tested to see if they have the required qualities. They must be able to put aside personal ambition and set themselves to serve the future without expectation of reward. Gurdjieff once said that two hundred conscious people could stop war. If this number will be available by 1990, the disaster that threatens mankind will be averted.

Finally, there is the true esoteric work, which is supernatural. There is at this present time a great spiritualizing action that is preparing the New Epoch. This action comes, as Gurdjieff puts it, "from

Above." All we can do is to cooperate with it and be its instruments. The spirit cannot work without the flesh. The New World communities are the flesh of the new humanity. Spiritual energies are its blood. But its life is entering from Above. I have confidence that this action will succeed so that many of you will see the birth of the New World.

Already there are communities that have the power to maintain their own potential and that do not depend upon an input of external energies to the same extent. External energies are needed for the maintenance of life and not for the stimulation of activity. These are "work communities." It is very likely that such communities, small and insignificant though they appear to be at this time, are the precursors of the new society.

Up until now the aim of "work groups" has, singly, been to preserve their existence in neutral or sometimes hostile environments. Now they have to come out into the open, and a quite different attitude is needed.[7]

The tens of thousands of small communities all over the world are trying to experiment with new ways of life, but most of them are failing. This is because they do not have the essential "know-how." There is something very difficult to accomplish, but this operation is being directed by a higher power and wisdom, and our part in it is more cooperation than innovation. It is being shown to the world what has to be done. The difficulty is that people cannot see what is being shown to them, and they do not know how to do what is required.

It is an extraordinary operation. The societies of the past four thousand years, with few exceptions, have been based upon egoism and more on the desire for greater personal satisfaction than the desire for service. At moments of great necessity, non-self-seeking societies have appeared, such as the Khwajagan* in central Asia or the monastic orders in Europe, but they have been local phenomena. Now the need is global, and not for a very, very long time has mankind required a new kind of structure, a new way of life.

The Shivapuri Baba** said, "This civilization has failed mankind. It will be swept away. It cannot give what mankind needs." He also said that two-thirds of the human race will perish, but I do not think this is probable in the literal sense, only in the sense that the majority of the human race will cease to be significant because they belong to a perished world, unable to adapt, and they will lose out.

We have been making experiments with a new way of life. Many

*The reader is referred to J.G. Bennett, *The Masters of Wisdom.*
**Long Pilgrimage. See Bibliography.

of us here now see for ourselves how difficult it is to change one's attitude from being centered on one's own rights, making demands, taking, and assuring one's own welfare to being centered on service. There is an obligation to fulfill in our living. This is not something imposed on us from outside, the whim of a creator, but something that arises from the needs of both this and higher worlds.

Gurdjieff's doctrine of "reciprocal maintenance" has to be translated into a form that can be easily understood, if not easily accepted.[8] We have to get it across that our life cannot be understood unless we take into account that everyone of us has a cosmic role to fulfill.

This idea can mean something to those who live under the idea of reward and punishment, heaven and hell. We can say that a certain way of life brings reward and another punishment. This is in the nature of things. People are also subject to the idea that we are entitled to get the best out of life for ourselves. Maybe it can be demonstrated that this is no longer possible if one man's hand is lifted against another, because of the closeness of our interaction.

We come back to the role of groups. There is a need to associate, a need for groups, but unless a group or community has a higher purpose, it is not possible for it to have equilibrium. If it is not a work group, it cannot maintain itself, because then the disruptive forces have nothing to balance them.

We cannot work alone. If someone who has been touched by this work does not realize it now, the time will come when he will realize it. There are ways that do not require working together, such as that of a hermit, but this is very difficult and rare. One must find people to share the Work with. At one time, this was very difficult, but now things have changed. There are more and more people who are receptive.

We do need to learn how to cooperate. When people are unsure of themselves and do not know what they are doing, then they are afraid that other people will misunderstand or spoil things. We must be able to work with people who also manifest the Work, though sometimes in quite a different form than our own way.

What is going to have to come is a new kind of "group consciousness." This is a sharing not only of the outward life but of the inner life—a real sharing. It is not from the inside to the outside and back inside again, but direct. This is needed for something beyond the requirements of group harmony, self-renewal, and establishing a higher level of energy, a conscious spiritual force. It is needed because of the change in the time scale of events brought about by the accelerated rate of change. It will be impossible for people to bear the world and its pressures as isolated individuals.

A group consciousness can have a different duration or "present moment" from an individual consciousness. It may well be that the world will move too fast for an individual to fulfill himself, and he will have to fulfill himself through a group. This will make human life very different from how it is now. The isolation and separateness of individuals will be very much less and the sense of unity within groups and communities very much more. There is some evidence that people more sensitive to that kind of awareness are being born in greater numbers, or greater proportion, than before. Some people speak of this as the birth of a new race, and this may be not altogether wrong.

Parenthood is becoming a much more significant factor in the life of the world than it has been in the recent past. This is connected with the possibility of a greater number of births of children with essences capable of developing new forms of consciousness. The parents of such children have themselves a cosmic responsibility.

We are now in the early stages of the development of group consciousness. It is very active below the surface, but there is little to be seen. We can look forward not only to a curtailment of individual isolation but also to a different kind of relationship between communities, one based on mutual support, not on power and authority.

The big institutions have little brains, and it is not difficult to outwit them. It is possible for the new society to begin to take shape within the existing society without attracting opposition if it is done intelligently.

Within a generation or two, I believe, the present institutions of government and large productive enterprises will give way to organizations the main purpose of which is just to ensure the exchange of necessities of life: food, commodities, and transport. They will be much less concerned with the production of things for the individual and much less concerned with the domination of the institution over the individual. This will bring human life toward a nonhierarchical harmony, just as the body is a nonhierarchical society that works because there is a life force that flows through it that enables each part to fulfill its purpose in relation to the whole. If only we could look into our bodies and talk intimately to our limbs and organs and all the systems of the body we would see that the real concern of every part is service to the whole. This is the direction that things will go, only not without much difficulty. The old institutions will continue and will resist change even when it is seen that they are moribund and doomed to extinction.

There are three things we need to ask ourselves. First, are we prepared to accept the principle that we live in order to fulfill a cosmic purpose and that it is only by this fulfillment that we can assure our own welfare? Second, do we accept that we cannot do things alone and that we need each other? Third, do we accept that a group consciousness is needed that is not just self-sustaining on the level of survival but self-sustaining on the suprasurvival level of creativity? If we do accept these things, then it is possible to see how the picture is to be translated into practical terms. But if we do not, then we can do only as we think best, and this may not work. If what we undertake does correspond to the cosmic situation, then the chances of its working are incomparably greater, because we shall then be working with the forces that are directing the evolution of the world.

DISCUSSION

[This discussion is taken from a meeting between Mr. Bennett and students of the Second Basic Course at the International Academy for Continuous Education, Sherborne House, Gloucestershire, England. *See also* appendix B: Inaugural Address, Second Basic Course, 1972–73. The reader may want to read appendix B before continuing on. The Sherborne Academy inaugural address, reprinted there, will give the reader a rich taste of life at the academy and will serve as an introduction to the discussion below.]

Student A.   When I first came, I wanted to find out all that was here, what the possibilities were. Now I find myself in the predicament where the more I feel in the way of ideas, the more confusing it becomes for me. None of the "morning exercises"[9] has any weight for me. I could not talk about or convey the psychological ideas. I can plant potatoes, but when it comes to ideas . . .

J.G. Bennett.   This work does not act uniformly on all people. Can you give it all up?

A.   Not for a minute—I can't give it up. It's got me; I haven't got it.

JGB.   Your situation isn't so bad. You see, no two people have responded in the same way to what has been done here. This is the best evidence that it is something authentic. Your response is your own response. It's the right one for you. It is right that you should be questioning, doubting, and not prepared to do something you don't understand. But this does not mean that you can go away and just plod on with what you have learned. You can experiment. You can say, "I don't know whether in the least I can help people, or get anything across to people, but I can at least try." In fact, you are less likely to make mistakes than somebody who thinks that they can do it all—only it will be very difficult for you, because you never believe that anyone has understood what you have said to them.

Student B. Some of us have been involved with people who worked in a certain way. How should we be related to them?
JGB. There is no general rule. People who have been accustomed to learning this work in a certain way and teaching it to others in the same way believe it to be the only way, and for them it is very difficult. There are others who are anxious to try anything new wherever it comes from, but it is not just with these that we shall have to work. Some very good people with long experience can teach the Work extraordinarily well in their own way, but they have not become aware of the change in climate. They have become accustomed to think of the Work as something esoteric, for the few. They do not see that the world situation has gone past that point.

Student C. There does seem to be a pattern of people looking for life in small communities.
JGB. At present, largely out of revolt against the kind of institutions that now dominate our life, people who are experimenting with small communities do so because they are looking for a better way of life. They are not looking at it as a necessity, as the only way of surviving.

There will be a time when people will begin to say about the world, "This is not working. We are not going to be able to go on like this. We must have something different," not "I don't like it. I'm going away with a few friends to form a community." If that happens, then people will be more ready to notice if there is anything that does work, and then they will say, "We must do something like that."

Very few of the tens of thousands of communities understand what they have set themselves to do and what one is up against when one tries to found a community not on authority, not on expansion, and not on trying to be more or better than others, but on quality. Then suppose some people say, "We are inviting people to come and join us who are prepared to think of quality alone and forget about quantity. We are going to have a hundred people who are going to set themselves as their only aim a quality of living." With that alone, it will not work. It does not take into account something in man that spoils things, that will make what he does become its own opposite.

Student D. What sort of motivation is needed for a community to work?

JGB. Where there is some motivation that is not just to have a community, it can work. It cannot work if one says, "Let us have a community. It is a desirable thing. Let us achieve this desirable thing together." History shows that this does not work. But if people say that there is something to be done, and if they all know that for it to be done it requires a community, then it can work.

Student E. I don't think that the political leaders will abdicate their roles so easily. I think somehow we are going to have to face up to the fact that political power can make or break this kind of thing.

JGB. We have to be clever little mice so that the dinosaurs will not notice. Governments are concerned only with their own survival. They turn against a movement only if they think that it might threaten their power. There was a tremendous reaction against political activism for the single reason that it was threatening the power of big organizations. It is not a question of government and big business abdicating their power. It wouldn't be good even if they did. The structure of society needs to hold together as long as it can . . . until something else is ready to take over. Of course, the powerful will not abdicate their power. At the moment, they are concentrating more power into their hands because they believe that there is no other way to make the world work. And at this moment they are quite right.

E. But what happens when things really break down?

JGB. This is what Beelzebub was often talking about. Beelzebub had seen a lot of the world, but he had not seen 1970! There is something coming that is totally different from anything in recorded history. The situation has got out of control. Nobody can do anything any longer. There is no power by which the thing can be put back on its rails. Anything that can be done happens so slowly that by the time it is half done it is no longer relevant. In any case, people do not know what to do or how to do it. It may have happened like this ten or a hundred thousand years ago, but we do not know what actually took place then.

Student F. What some of us are feeling is that the Work rouses up the "denying force" and there must be some kind of conflict.

JGB. The denying force is now so overwhelming that human affirmation is really snuffed out. The forces at work are on a very great scale—including the reconciling force of the Work.[10] This force is not just all the different people who work on themselves; there is something very much greater working. This does not mean that some people will not be martyred in the process. Martyrs are, in fact, necessary. There are certain energies that cannot be made available except through a special kind of suffering.

If we look at the situation as a whole, mankind should be saved, and this is worth a few worthy beings.*

Student G. Do you have any idea what it will be like in the next century?

JGB. You think I can put on my heavenly eye and look a century forward and tell you all about it! I must say that what I see when I look is unexpected to me. What I see is not the disappearance of large organizations but that a kind of cooperation will arise. The need for communities will be so evident that they will be accepted, and people who can produce viable communities will be accepted. This is in fifty years' time. At the same time, on account of the complexity of the world, large institutions will be needed. There will be a kind of symbiosis for a considerable time.

---

*In later years, Bennett modified this view. Cf. *Masters of Wisdom*, chap. 5 (London: Turnstone Press, 1976). [Note from original edition.]

IT MAY BE that the future of life as a whole is more important than the future of man, and there may be demiurgic powers whose task it is to see that life is not wantonly dismembered by the human race. If so, those intelligences can certainly find means to keep human wantonness in check and eventually prepare a new race to take our place if we have to be removed from the face of the earth.

Chapter 2

Spiritual Community

Part 1. HAZARD AND UNCERTAINTY

THERE IS THE CONDITIONED and the unconditioned, the world of common experience and the other that is nonmaterial. Neither of them is complete without the other. As a painter is not a painter without canvas and colors, so the canvas is not a picture until it is painted on. Will has no existence, but will is not important without existence as its field of action and instrument of operation, and existence is dead and useless unless it is penetrated by the will. Because of this interdependence, we can talk of the "third realm of realization," or fulfillment. Existence realizes itself by transcending itself. Nonexistence realizes itself by sacrificing some of its unconditioned freedom.[1]

The conditioned realm contains many things that we ordinarily think of as unconditioned: mind and feeling, potentialities not actualized, patterns of possibilities, and other seemingly "immaterial" entities.* These things exist in the dimension of "eternity."[2] Just as there is no timeless existence and no existence out of space, so every moment at all times and in all places is accompanied by a pattern of potentialities and forms and meanings that are eternal.

Every moment also includes interaction with its discontinuities and hazards. This is as true for the level of causal actualization, where the potential may even be single valued as it is for the regions of the finest materiality. Every moment, large or small, of the existing world is in contact with the unconditioned world of will. The present moment is any region of the existing world that is in correspondence with one will.

Discontinuity and hazard belong to the dimension of "hyparxis."[3] We can agree to the theistic doctrine that the entire existing universe throughout all space and time is the present moment of the Supreme

*These belong to the spirit world. In later years Bennett spoke of two conditioned worlds: the physical and the spirit. There are also two unconditioned worlds: the spiritual and the unfathomable. [Note from original edition.]

Will, but hyparxis precludes the predetermination of existence.

Within every present moment, from that of the smallest, most transient will to that of the Will of the unconditioned realm, there are discontinuities and uncertainties. We can go further and assert that the greater the present moment, the greater the hazard.

Complexity must increase at a faster rate than proliferation; that is, there are always more relationships than there are entities as soon as the number goes beyond three. With three billion people living on the earth today [1968], there are factorial 3×10^9 primary relationships: a number beside which the count of all the atoms of the universe is a handful. By contemplating such enormous numbers, we can form some idea of the degree of uncertainty that interaction introduces into the existing world. The future is unpredictable on every scale but most unpredictable on the greatest. If there is some contrary principle by which hazard is dominated, this principle must operate transcendentally, that is, from beyond existence.

There is nothing that science or philosophy can say for or against this. We must draw the conclusion that within the universe all is subject to hazard, and the universal drama is objectively as well as subjectively present to every conscious will. Science and philosophy can go no further: if God is beyond hazard, only his revelation can make this known within the world. This conclusion contradicts the supposition that the human reason can pronounce upon the First Cause. We must, however, insist that under the conditions of existence, hazard there must be.

We can and must go further than this and affirm that hazard is the very measure by which this Will can act within the world. The one attribute of God that even the simplest faith discovers is love. If we examine, not merely human love as it is manifested in our experience, but love in the most complete and all-embracing sense that we can imagine, it is impossible to picture its operation in the absence of hazard. All human virtues and values require hazard for their manifestation. It is also evident that without hazard there would be no place for hope. Faith links the two worlds, assuring us that the conditioned existence can look beyond itself to what it cannot perceive or even understand. Neither hope nor faith could have any meaning for the unconditioned will, as Saint Paul says in other and more eloquent words in 1 Corinthians, chapter 15. Indeed, faith triumphs in the straitjacket of the stubborn fact where all the evidence contradicts the reality of the unconditioned Will, and man and nature appear to be will-less mechanisms.

Love is entirely different. Love flourishes in uncertainty and hazard yet by its very nature is unconditioned. It is unconditioned, but it has no mission in the unconditioned world; to manifest, it must enter into existence, where it is needed. It seems to me a self-evident truth that the greater the hazard, the greater the love that it can evoke. So intimately linked are love and hazard that we cannot conceive of either without the other.

It would be possible, I believe, to base the entire argument for the universality of hazard as a condition of existence upon the assurance that love is a reality and must have an unlimited field in which to give itself. These last words are the key to completing our model. In order "to give" there must be a recipient, and this means a void place, a discontinuity. There would be no point of entry for love into the existing world unless the dimension of hyparxis lay adjacent to the unconditioned.

We need not identify the sixth dimension with the World of Realization, but we can say that it leads into it. For reasons we cannot go into here, I have been led to postulate a direction that leads out of the present moment—like time leads out of the past and into the future—toward an unconditioned state. I have called this the Hyparchic Future,[4] and I would say that this is within the World of Realization. The peculiar character of the Hyparchic Future is that it is a state of existence in which nothing has yet become actual and potentialities can be freely created. It is not timeless, and so experience can be like that in our present moment except that there is no causality and, therefore, every moment is freely open to the Supreme Will. Its hyparchic character lies in that it is a discontinuity within the existing world but an unlimited discontinuity open freely to the unconditioned.

Part 2. TRANSFORMATION AND SIN

THESE IDEAS MAY SEEM EASY to grasp; in reality they can be understood only by analogy, because the human mind is unable to think unconditionally. If we succeed in forming some conception of the Hyparchic Future, it will be from the perspective of "existence."[5] We must suppose that the World of Realization is more concrete, more *real,* than the World of Existence, because in it the conditioned and unconditioned achieve unity in a higher synthesis of which we have only glimpses. This synthesis is what I mean by *transformation.* As a process in time, it is the penetrating, step by step, of the Individual Will into the human selfhood, until a moment comes when the conditioned state gives way and the transformed human person enters into the beatific vision of the unconditioned Lord.

The same word *transformation* applies with exactly the same meaning to the evolution of life on earth. Life is visibly populating the surface of the existing earth. It is also invisibly making its way into the World of Realization. One of the most terrifying mistakes made by man is to regard other forms of life as having no more than an economic or, at best, a sentimental value. Man is not independent of life. All life is one whole body in which mankind should be the seat of consciousness and creativity and the instrument of the Will. But however high and, indeed, unique man's present status may be, he cannot repudiate the life from which he sprang without losing the purpose of his own existence.

Atheistic biologists have said that from now on the evolution of life on the earth depends more upon man than upon natural selection. This is true, but not for the reason they suppose. It is because the demiurgic responsibilities must be—and are being—transferred to man.[6] It will be very hard for people, concerned as they are with their own human welfare, to realize that they must serve life and not enslave it. Albert Schweitzer, one of the forerunners of the New Epoch and a great prophet, saw this and proclaimed it. But his was a voice crying in the wilderness, to which scant attention was paid. The lovers of living things do what they can, but the insatiable flood of human demands sweeps all before it.

The evolution of life is not ended. New forms will appear— including new species of Homo. Already there are evidences of mutations that will survive with the protection now available. These mutants are unlikely to develop very far at the present stage and will be regarded as freaks or geniuses. The time will come when men with new powers of perception will be born and multiply, and they will have a different capacity for interaction. The time scales will change, and men will begin to think in terms of centuries or even millennia, not, as at present, within the span of their own active lives.

But the new forms of life will not be human only, and they may not appear until man has learned to respect life better. Or it may also be that they will appear in the form of deadly organisms that will destroy much human life to make way for a better and more balanced world. It may be that the future of life as a whole is more important than the future of man, and there may be demiurgic powers whose task it is to see that life is not wantonly dismembered by the human race. If so, those intelligences can certainly find means to keep human wantonness in check and eventually prepare a new race to take our place if we have to be removed from the face of the earth. These are all possibilities that should make us cautious in forecasting the future in terms of what we see about us today.

These apocalyptic musings should not be disregarded in our search for an understanding of the situation of humanity and our own. We are bound to have sin and evil in our minds as we look at the load of suffering under which so much of humanity is bowed. Psychology, physiology, and biochemistry have combined to destroy the simple picture of man as a responsible being whose disobedience to God's command was sin and the cause of his mortality. We know that men can be conditioned without their knowledge to believe monstrous fiction and to commit abominations. We know that chemically active substances will turn a mild man into a murderer and that, conversely, drugs will remove all initiative and make the wildest savage into a harmless automaton. We know that there are hidden mechanisms that control behavior and for which it is impossible to hold the conscious mind responsible. And yet, with all this, we cannot feel that mankind is guiltless in the massive indifference to suffering and the egoism that poisons personal relationships.

It is fashionable now to deny the reality of sin and evil and yet to blame others for doing what we disapprove of. This strangely inconsistent attitude has come about because we simply do not understand man—either his nature or his destiny. When man was endowed with creativity—a critical event in history that I believe occurred during the last Ice Age—a great risk was taken, and something went wrong. Whereas animals may be cruel or wanton, they do not act against their nature. Man, on the contrary, acts, as we ourselves say, "inhumanly," especially in his dealings with other men. Man has an individual will, which has been placed in him for a very high purpose, the realization of which requires that he should unite in harmonious action with other men. Eventually this separate will must reunite with the source from which it came. Man has come to regard himself as fundamentally free from obligations except to himself and possibly to his fellow men. This is a very strange attitude in a being who cannot possibly by his own powers achieve the freedom from conditioning that he thinks he has a right to.

Man is like a child who insists upon using some dangerous weapon and will not even allow his elders to show him how it works.

We should not call this "sin," because we do not demand responsible action from a child. But are we to absolve humanity from all responsibility for the misery of the world on the grounds of immaturity? If not, may we do so on the plea that man is the slave of his own chemistry and cannot control his behavior even if he sees that it will bring trouble on himself?

It seems that any of these arguments must, in the end, come to the denial that man has a will and, with that, to the denial that there is a Supreme Will. The two denials, as Kant saw, are inseparable. If there are not obligations that man both can and must fulfill, then we have no grounds for believing in God. It is just because the sense of obligation is clouded that the present generation of humanity has become more irreligious than in any previous time in recorded history. And yet the obligation remains, and no one escapes it—even by biochemical devices. Man can deny obligation only by denying that he has will, that is, by denying that he is a man—and it is doubtful if anyone can succeed in doing this. Making excuses and blaming anything and everyone is another matter: this we are all good at. We may refuse to blame ourselves at all, but we will not go so far as to say that we are animals and nothing more.

In some way it has been revealed to man that he is more than an animal and that he is capable of acts of will, and he can never wholly repudiate this revelation. For this reason, sin is and must be willful and not involuntary. There is in every man a link with the Cosmic Individuality, that is, with Christ, and this link is not wholly hidden from any of us, although we may be very far from being conscious of its significance. The categorical imperative is the demand made on us by our link with the Perfect Man, and we have an instrument, moral conscience, that tells us when we have defaced the image. Therefore, no one can deny the reality of sin except by verbal subtleties that seem to destroy the meaning of the term. No subtleties can destroy the awareness of obligation that challenges our will to accept or reject it.

This long digression was unavoidable because of the equivocal attitude of so many people toward sin and evil. Let us now go forward on the hypothesis that sin is a reality and that it has interposed a special kind of obstacle in the way of man's communication with the unconditioned world. If sin is a particular form of conditioning that prevents man from seeing that the hazards of his existence are the means by which he can fulfill his destiny, it follows that man will see hazard as a misfortune rather than as an opportunity and will seek to close the door to freedom rather than keep it open. In its simplest form, this leads to an assessment of experience in terms of pleasure and pain, labeled as "happiness" and "suffering." We do not wish to suffer because we "cannot see the point of it." In a deeper and even more significant interpretation, we reject the necessity for sacrifice because it appears to be a demand made upon us from without, instead of being a requirement of self-realization.

Our model of the world enables us to give an objective account of sin in terms of transformation. We postulate an aim or purpose that is shared by the conditioned and the unconditioned worlds: to achieve "realization" by the union of "will" and "existence." Sin is the refusal to serve this aim when the opportunity to do so arises for us. Sin opts out of the process, because the sinner refuses to pay the price, which is the submission of his own will to the divine purpose. The consequences of opting out are deadly serious, for it means that the sinner cuts himself off from the reality toward which all existence is striving. He gets left behind. This is to be taken in a literal sense that never occurs to people: he falls out of the stream of evolution and gets into the past, where realization has ceased.

There would be little hope for any of us if we were obliged to keep up with the inexorable march of time with no hope of "getting a lift" if we stumbled. The situation is not like this, for the present moment of the world is large enough to leave room for many starts and stops without our being eliminated from the race. It still remains true, however, that it is possible to lose one's place and be unable to catch up. In one form or another, both as religious dogma and as a commonly accepted attitude toward death, the belief has been held in the past that there is a state of existence that is less substantial and with fewer possibilities of free choice than this present life. "Descending into the shades" is an expression common from China to Europe and Africa. There is also a widespread belief that souls that have fallen out of the stream and have been caught in the shadowy state will be set free "at the end of time."

All such ideas tend nowadays to be rejected as "primitive" in favor of one or two positions. Either existence after death is denied as impossible, or it is accepted but looked at in far more optimistic terms as a kind of improved version of this present life. Both positions are incompatible with the hypothesis of transformation. If transformation is possible and yet not guaranteed, then we live in a condition of hazard. The hazard may be the simple one of succeeding or not succeeding in attaining individuation, or it may be complicated by the burden of sin. We may have an inherited tendency to refuse to pay the price for the transformation of selfhood into individuality, which price in the long run amounts to the sacrifice of egoism.

Part 3. THE ROLE OF LOVE
AND THE PATH OF SANCTIFICATION

WHEN WE CONTEMPLATE the terrifying picture of man congenitally handicapped in the already hazardous pursuit of reality, we are brought sharply back to our fundamental dependence upon love. Without love, no way out could open except for those few heroic souls who of their own volition were able to sacrifice existence to attain reality. I have distinguished between conditioned love within the existing world and unconditioned love, which is an attribute of God. Within the world we can help one another. The strong can help the weak, and what one cannot do alone may be possible for several wills in unison. No one doubts that human nature demands that the strong should help the weak, but generally speaking, all are weak in meeting the requirements of transformation.

This brings us to the notions of redemption and salvation and particularly to the Christian doctrine of the incarnation of God to deliver mankind from the consequences of inherited sin. The missions of God in the world are creative, redemptive, and enabling, represented by the Three Persons of the Christian Trinity. As I am not competent to discuss theological questions, I must leave these matters of doctrine with the observation that nothing in our model of the world seems to be incompatible with the belief that God acts in the world as a creative power, as the word of wisdom and salvation, and as the spirit of love and reconciliation.

There is, however, one very important point of interpretation. It is that any operations—including divine operations—within the existing world must be subject to the determining conditions of existence itself. This seems particularly necessary for any reasonable understanding of the doctrine of redemption. If we disregard the limitations that enter from the very existence of existence, it would be possible by decree of the transcendental Godhead to put time back to the moment when sin entered human nature and, allowing man the benefit of insight, to give him "another chance." It would also be possible to wipe out the consequences of the past by changing the entire pattern of potentialities accompanying the human race. If we hold to the principle that such acts would be against God's nature as destroying what he had created, we must also accept all the other limitations that are inherent in the existence of existence. This being so, the world could not have been redeemed except by a sacrifice made within the world, at the very point at which the break with the Supreme Will had been made, that is, in the human selfhood.

If we are to remain faithful to our principle, we must hold that the incarnation [of Christ] itself was a hazardous undertaking. This seems to be confirmed by the entire tenor of the Gospels, which at no point show the mission of Christ as assured of success. On the contrary, the prophetic utterances of Jesus were anything but reassuring as to the future of mankind. The subsequent history of two thousand years has demonstrated that although the consequences of sin had been neutralized by the sacrifice of Calvary, the tendency to sin continued to operate unchanged in all but a few of the followers of Jesus.

The love of God entered humanity with Pentecost, and those who could respond acquired a new quality far higher than creativity; this quality is "sanctity," or union of the individual will with the will of God. The saint is a man whose transformation has been completed during his earthly life and who is free from the determining conditions so far as his selfhood is concerned. In a very important sense he has ceased to exist, because his actions no longer belong to the conditioned world but to the World of Realization.

The saint can outstrip time and enter the Hyparchic Future, from which he is able to inject new potentialities into the present moment of the world. He now has powers that we have previously associated with the demiurgic intelligences, but he is totally different in nature because they are unconditioned in their origin, whereas he is unconditioned by transformation. He may be more limited in the span of his will—the demiurgic intelligences may work in terms of millions of years—but he has acquired in his earthly life an experience of the conditioned world that intelligence alone cannot give.

I, myself, have no doubt of the reality of sanctification, and I believe that its importance for the world cannot be overstressed. There are many paths of transformation—not all of them religious and not all even aiming specifically at transformation—and not all people who are capable of following them become aware of the possibility.

Part 4. SPIRITUAL COMMUNITY

IN THE DRAMATIC UNIVERSE I divided mankind into three groups: psychostatic, psychokinetic, and psychotelios. The psychostatic group consists of those whose potential does not extend beyond their present moment. They must evolve with humanity. They are necessary people, and their role in the world is not to be despised. They do not aspire to transformation, and if they are content to fill the role that corresponds to their destiny, they are safely carried along with the mainstream of human evolution.

The psychokinetic group is made up of those who have entered into the process of transformation. These are involved in the hazards of the world. They cannot know their goal or their own potentialities, and they have no assurance of a successful outcome of their striving.

They have to find the unconditioned through the conditioned, that is, through the gaps and discontinuities of hyparxis. Whatever path they may follow, they cannot come to the end of it without suffering and sacrifice. It is normal for psychokinetic people to occupy positions of responsibility, though not of power, for they can have a more independent judgment and greater freedom from subject influences than psychostatic people.

The psychotelios group includes different categories of saints or transformed people. They cannot be understood by men still living wholly in the conditioned world. Their behavior is unaccountable. They may occupy any worldly position or none. They are all united in will with the Unconditioned Will and therefore with one another. Without contact or communication, they are channels for the concentration and distribution of creative energy that renews the conscious life of mankind, and for this reason I have called them the "Hidden Directorate." They do nothing of themselves, for they are free from egoism in their selfhood and from the influences of their environment because they have been set free from the determining conditions not only in their wills but in their souls also.

The saints, having outstripped time, are also called the "results of accelerated transformation." This means that they reach, while still living in a physical body, the stage of development toward which mankind is moving and is destined to reach in the remote future. People of the psychokinetic group may not complete their transformation during this life, but the process, once initiated, does not end with death. Religion teaches the doctrine of purgatory on the freeing of souls from the consequences of their past lives under special conditions of existence after death. It seems that we can identify the purgatorial state as the region common to eternity and hyparxis and out of space-time. No other set of conditions would allow potentialities to be modified without actualization. The transition region has the peculiar property of being stationary for time; nothing at all happens there, and yet it allows decision: abandonment of attachment to conditioned existence.

There is, then, nothing in the traditional doctrine of purgatory that does not fit into our model. The interpretation is, however, substantially different from the common belief that access to purgatory is an easy matter, open to any soul without mortal sin. As we understand transformation to mean *complete liberation of the will from its attachment to the existing world* and, in addition, *the purification of the soul so that it is exempt from the determining conditions,* we are bound to include that the purgatorial state represents an advanced stage of transformation accessible only to souls already strong enough to bear the extreme tension of the boundary region.

If this is not evident, I should explain that every boundary region is a limiting condition. For example, the boundary between space and time is marked by the limiting velocity of light. In order to enter this region a particle must lose all its mass. The boundary between time and eternity is marked by the limit of actualization. A body can pass from time to eternity only by ceasing to actualize. When visible motion turns into invisible potential, the transition concerns the energy of motion only, but when a particle "dematerializes," an enormous transformation of energy is involved. When we pass through the crisis of conscience, our being seems to disintegrate and all seems lost. We must expect that the purgatorial transformation must require a far greater tension in the soul.

From this excursion into the interpretation of our cosmic model we infer that accelerated transformation by way of purgatory is the destiny of strong and pure souls, and this raises the question as to what happens to ordinary "good" people. Once again, our model suggests that "merit" as acquired during life takes the form of "potential existence" and therefore does not degenerate with time. Such "merit" is derived exclusively from acts of will. All other actions are the result of pre-existing causes, that is, of conditioning, and their results must be confined to the conditioned world.

Here an important psychological point arises. We might suppose that an "act of will" means an action performed intentionally and consciously. We must distinguish between an act that is unconditioned and an action that is within the existing world. An *act* may influence an entire sequence of actions and change the course of our lives, but it is not itself a process in time and space. It is the insertion of a new factor into the existing world at a point where there is a hyparchic discontinuity. The "act of will" is a commitment to action, not the act itself. The commitment is transmitted into the existing world by the creative energy, which can initiate new processes of interaction between man and his world.

This is why soul making has been rightly compared to procreation and the formation of the soul has been called "rebirth." Every man during his life makes or mars his soul stuff, and the resulting soul passes at death into a state of potentiality. There is a gamut of possibilities, ranging from almost complete conditioning to almost complete freedom. At one extreme, the soul remains attached to its space-time existence. At the other, it is wholly committed to liberation and enters the purgatorial zone, which will lead it into the Hyparchic Future, where its evolution has no limits. This is the state of sanctification, and it is of the utmost importance for the evolution of mankind that there should be saints enough in the world to transmit the help that is needed to compensate for innumerable failures to accept hazard positively by way of sacrifice rather than to seek escape by avoidance.

The role of men and women, transformed or in the way of transformation, is not confined to their unseen hyparchic commitment. They are required to support the transformation of those weaker than themselves. Some of them become focal points round which a few or many others can come together and open a path into the regions of higher potentiality. It is very necessary to distinguish between those who attempt such a task relying on their own strength and those who are aware that they can do nothing without the help of the Unconditioned Will. The first are false prophets who deceive themselves and others. The second kind belong—consciously or unconsciously—to the future soul of humanity, called the Communion of Saints.

This brings us back to the purpose of it all. Mankind is still divided and enslaved by the illusion that existence is the sole reality. The sin of pride that separates man from his source is now, as it always has been, the enemy of man's transformation.

The way of salvation has been revealed, but man will not take it unless he is awakened to the reality of his situation. We are now at a time of change. Man has never been more powerful and more helpless than he is in the twentieth century. The instruments of government—

democracies and oligarchies—that have been built up over the centuries are failing. New forces are being concentrated in unexpected places: power is passing to the great international corporations that control the productive capacity upon which the lives of people depend. If rightly directed, these new forces can prevent wars and bring about an equitable distribution of the world's resources. They have an advantage over the existing forms of government in that they are more able to take commitments on a scale commensurate, in time and extent, with the needs of the modern world. This is not to say that they are good decision makers, but already they are more effective than governments.

The reservation just made that these new forces must be "rightly directed" brings us to the question "What form of society on the earth corresponds to the true destiny of mankind?" Some people place their hope in a "world government," failing to see that centralized authority must be conditioned by the circumstances of interaction and communication. Very limited knowledge of human organizations is enough to convince us that no centralized authority can maintain social harmony. The Platonic vision of states ruled by philosopher kings can never become actual, because the exercise of power and the detachment required in a true philosopher are incompatible; exactly the contrary is required. Each of the three orders of people—distinguished not in terms of their conditioned qualities but of their state of transformation—is required for the future evolution of mankind.

Right direction comes from the transformed men whose will and creative power are wholly free from conditioning, but for this very reason they cannot communicate with those who are wholly involved in the conditioned state of existence. This is why the psychokinetic group—the people in process of transformation—have a vital role to play. They cannot devote themselves exclusively to their own liberation because that would cut them off from the very purpose of their existence, which is to serve the world and not to escape from it. They are the channels of communication by which the world can profit from the wisdom and the blessings of the saints.

In the past, human societies have for brief periods organized themselves on these principles. These are called "theocratic states" to indicate that they accept the Supreme Will as the only authority to be obeyed. These states have not maintained their ideal for long chiefly because of the lack of psychokinetic channels and the inability of the rulers to discriminate between true and false prophets.

The world is beginning to see that those who are able to gain power over others cannot have the wisdom to use it rightly. They cannot because if they were wise, they would avoid power like the plague, understanding—as truly wise people do—that the exercise of power is a conditioning process that obstructs transformation. It should, therefore, be left to the psychostatic group, but the prevailing notion that the acquisition of wealth and power and the exercise of authority are superior functions must be discredited.

A remarkable and hopeful feature of our time is the changing attitude toward power in large organizations. It is seen to be undesirable that authority and power should be vested in one man or a ruling oligarchy. Decisions are taken by agreement, and "experts" are entrusted with preparing them. Though still far from the true relationship, this is at least a move toward the recognition that people with special training should advise and be listened to but not rule or exercise authority. It is also recognized now that the expert advisers should not be technicians only—the vogue of technocracy did not last long—but specialists in all fields, including human relationships. All this may be looked upon as the material outcome of competition and the drive to greater efficiency, but it also may be due to unseen influences preparing the way for a new social structure corresponding to the needs of mankind in the next stage of evolution.

This next stage will be one of greater organization. There will be larger societies with more complex interactions, and, consequently, hazard must increase. There are natural hazards and there are human hazards, and there are also artificial hazards resulting from man-made constructions. All of these will operate on a larger scale and with longer-range consequences than in former times when humanity had not acquired its present powers of communication and transport and its control over the energies of nature. These hazards cannot be met by human wisdom alone, and we must confidently look for intervention from the unconditioned world.

It is indispensable for humanity that the religious sense of dependence upon God and "his Word made manifest" should be restored. We can see evidence that—against the expectations of the majority of students of human history—this is coming about in spite of rather than by the endeavors of man.

We can already discern the outlines of the future universal church. It will not, as in the past, be another worldly church, but one whose mission will be to keep open the channels of communication between the World of Existence and the World of Will. It will be first a sacramental church, by which I understand one that is the instrument whereby the Unconditioned Will acts upon the wills of men to liberate them from the consequences of sin, to bring their individuality into communion with Christ, and to give them the means of sanctification. It will be seen that sanctification is a transformation that can proceed along many paths, all having in common the service to humanity and the liberation of the selfhood from egoism, which are the two conditions whereby the soul can acquire strength and purity to endure purgation.

All these characteristics are already present in the universal Catholic church, and some of them are present in a great number of religious communities, Christian and non-Christian. They need and will receive new interpretations in accordance with the needs of the coming age of mankind. These new interpretations will remove many illusory barriers and awaken hopes. They will not change the fundamental character of this world, with the determining conditions that allow it to exist. Until the World of Realization can take in and unite the two that are now separate, limitation and hazard will continue to prevail. The World of Realization is both the kingdom of heaven and the kingdom of God upon earth, for it unites the unconditioned and the conditioned states in a new creation. That world is not the remote future but here and now for those who can follow the path of sanctification through to the end.

✧

IT IS AN INTEGRAL and essential part of the psychokinetic attitude toward life that we need and can count on help "from Above." Communication with higher worlds is very much dependent on how we are with each other.

The act of worship and certain manifestations that are called ritual enable a certain state of energy to be created in which the whole process of transformation is enormously reinforced. These things cannot happen unless there is full confidence between people.

Chapter 3

Three Orders of Human Society

I HAVE DIVIDED MANKIND into three orders of people: *psychostatic,* those who are not concerned with any movement of the soul, who are content to remain inwardly the same and look for all change outside themselves; *psychokinetic,* those who are on the way, in search of a soul and in process of transformation, which in Gurdjieff's language means those who accept to live according to *parktdolg duty;*[1] and *psychotelios*, those whose transformation has already been completed. When I speak of an ideal society, I mean that those would be admitted who were determined to enter in the psychokinetic path. They would remain in the ideal society as long as they were upon the path. Such a society would correspond to what is said in the "organization for man's existence according to Ashiata Shiemash."[2]

Each of the three orders should contain four subgroups to keep things in balance. In the psychostatic order there are *dependents, producers, craftsmen,* and *leaders.*

Dependents are those who cannot provide for themselves either materially or spiritually through their own initiative. There will always be in mankind those who are dependent. Nature works so that there is not uniformity. There can be people with exceptional potential and people with minimal potential. The role of dependents is an essential one in a society because they are the ones the others can serve and take care of, as we do with children.

Producers are those without initiative who are nevertheless able to work. They are outwardly independent but inwardly dependent. They can produce their own requirements but cannot create their own opportunities.

Craftsmen are those who are able to create opportunities, who are inwardly independent but require the support of those who work, as in our present economic system.

39

Leaders are those able to exercise authority but who are not concerned with the transformation of their inner life.

In the psychokinetic order there are *candidates, specialists, counsellors,* and *initiates.*

Candidates are those who wish to enter the way but require teaching and external conditions. They do not know themselves, nor the way for themselves.

Specialists are those who have their inner vision open but only in a certain direction.

Counsellors are those who are capable of guiding others.

Initiates are those who have a direct perception and can receive guidance from the spiritual world.

A psychokinetic society that is not at least in connection with an initiated being will fail because it will not have a corrective for the mistakes that are made by those who are just specialists. The first two subgroups do not have direct access to spiritual knowledge, or a very precarious access, and they are liable to deceive themselves.

The essential idea of the psychokinetic order is that there is a progression of the soul. One will begin as a candidate and then discover one's particular aptitude, a particular kind of service one can make. In performing that service, one will be preparing oneself to receive insights and to awaken conscience. When conscience is really awakened, one passes over the "middle line," and then the center of gravity is the spiritual world and one's actions are directed from that world. This does not mean that there are not mistakes, but one is then able to guide others.

In the psychotelios order there are *saints, guides, prophets,* and *messengers.*

Saints: This is the highest level that can be reached by the development of an ordinary man. People reach the psychotelios order when their egoism dies. This is what Gurdjieff means in *Beelzebub's Tales** when he refers to someone as "now already a saint."

Guides: It is probably true that these guides were destined to be guides before they were born, but they still have to reach it by their own transformation.

Prophets: In the Bible there is a distinction between major and minor prophets. The major ones are sent from God. The top two levels of society are not reached by transformation from below. John

---

**All and Everything: An Objectively Impartial Criticism of the Life of Man, or Beelzebub's Tales to His Grandson* (New York: Harcourt, Brace & Company, Inc., 1950); (New York: E. P. Dutton & Co., Inc., 1964).

the Baptist was a prophet who was more than a prophet: "There was a man sent from God whose name was John" (John 1.6). It was also said, "Behold I send my messenger before thy face to prepare thy way before thee" (Mark 1.2). The picture of John the Baptist is of someone with his role already prepared from his mother's womb. Before he was born, he was able to recognize Christ: "The child of my womb leaps for joy" (Luke 1.44).

Messengers: The messenger is the very word of God and transmits a revelation.

An ideal society would have to be large enough to fulfill all the roles that are needed but not so large that mutual recognition and confidence of commitment to the psychokinetic path of transformation and service would be lost. Such a society would have a responsibility to the rest of the world, particularly the psychostatic order, from whom, after all, the candidates for the psychokinetic order are drawn. It would have to provide for its own dependents: first of all its children and then those who for reason of old age or illness were incapable of supporting themselves. It would also have to provide for its own maintenance and material support.

To remain at the stage of candidate is to stagnate. One has to pass through that. It is necessary to understand what it means to "create something of one's own."

This whole endeavor would be meaningless if there were not higher levels of being or a spiritual world. It is an integral and essential part of the psychokinetic attitude toward life that we need and can count on help "from Above." Communication with higher worlds is very much dependent on how we are with each other. The act of worship and certain manifestations that are called ritual enable a certain state of energy to be created in which the whole process of transformation is enormously reinforced. These things cannot happen unless there is full confidence between people.

There are ways of helping individuals overcome difficulties that are partly connected with their physical body and partly with their psychic nature. This can happen only when there are people who are on such a level of development that they can undertake such responsibilities for others. This is really the place of the healing specialist. A truly psychokinetic society contributes to the awakening of the spiritual awareness in the psychostatic society surrounding it.

The external form—and particularly the kind of material environment—depends on the needs of the people. If a temple were built, it would not be for the sake of having a temple but because the time had come when the society was able to worship in its own way. If a school were to be founded, it would be because it was then needed that the children should be brought up on psychokinetic principles.

Agriculture and care of the land would be conducted on the principle of reciprocal maintenance[3] with full regard to nature and not just to man and his needs. Such a kind of husbandry would be possible only in a psychokinetic society because it requires the sacrifice of some of the luxuries of life.

Of greatest importance would be the way in which authority is exercised. This should follow Ashiatan[4] principles: Authority is never taken by anyone, but, because they have exceptional qualities, it is imposed on them by others who make them stand out. A society like that is almost unknown. The nearest approximation to it is in the monasteries. But there there is another factor involving respect for age, so that the council of elders plays the major part in decision making.

A genuine psychokinetic society would take time to form just because time is needed for people to develop and to be recognized as having qualities by others. According to the Ashiatan principle, it is necessary to have people in a situation who, by their devoted acts toward their fellowmen, will stand out and will be listened to.

There are groups who do work of high excellence, such as the anthroposophists in education [Waldorf schools], but they are not listened to outside of their own people. It is the same with the Quaker schools.

The Fourth Way is a psychokinetic society that works on the principle of accelerated transformation. This idea was introduced by Gurdjieff and popularized by Ouspensky in his writings. There is also the perennial philosophy that says that the secrets of man's transformation are for the most part preserved in secret, but when something is required this is released for the fulfilling of a task. The Fourth Way is always associated with a task; it comes forward to do that task, and after completing it, it withdraws. There cannot be the right relationship between the psychostatic and psychokinetic orders unless a need is there that can provide something of a reconciliation. It is the *need* that changes everything and makes the Fourth Way possible.

✧

Chapter 4

The Spirit of a Society

WHEN THERE IS AN EVENT that becomes a whole, when something has been brought into realization, there exists something apart from the physical components. This is the spirit of the event. The spirit remains while the tangible phenomena perish.[1] That is why it is possible to enter into past events and experience them. There are places with a spirit, especially where some spiritual reality has come into being; that "being" is still there. This is quite different from the phenomena of memory, traces of the past, and what can be reconstructed from the material evidence.

I can give an example of what I am speaking about from my own experience. Some of us were visiting the Chateau of Anjou on the Loire in France, and we were waiting in one of the rooms for the guide to appear. I was overtaken by a terrible fear and misery. I could not understand what was happening to me. First I thought that I had eaten something that produced this state, but I had eaten only excellent French food, and nothing particularly unpleasant had happened to me that day. Then the guide came in and he told us that we were in the old torture chamber. I then realized that the place had an evil spirit in it, but beforehand I could not have known anything about this.

However, it is not a rule that all spirits have to do with this kind of agonizing experience. Sometimes there are very beautiful spirits.

I am saying this to try to convey to you that there really are in the spirit world counterparts of things that happen in this physical world, but the degree of coherence of the spirit counterpart depends upon the density and coherence of the event that transpires. Trivial events just evaporate, and nothing is left: the substance that surrounds them, which is a sensitive material, just blows away and disperses. Nontrivial events produce something stronger.

At the end of the eighteenth and the beginning of the nineteenth centuries, some German philosophers like Goethe took this into account in their understanding of history. They introduced the word

43

zeitgeist, spirit of the time, or spirit of the epoch. People did not grasp what they were saying because they did not have the concept of a dimension in which there could be such a kind of existence, where there is something made of energy but not in the way the physical world is made.[2] Finer energies are involved, but, more importantly, this mode of existence is not held together by the forces that have to work in the physical world to compensate for the effects of space and time: separateness and successiveness. In a world where there is not space and time as we know them, the requirements for holding together are different. It is very hard to form any idea of the spirit world, even for those who are convinced that some such world exists. Applied to history, the idea of a spirit world means that there can be some kind of organizing influence that forms the historical process.

I meant to talk about human societies. As I look at them, they are not something that is brought together through external forces or by attraction and then, after a time, disintegrates; rather, they are the manifestation of a spiritual pattern that forms the spirit of the society. The strength of the spirit determines the strength of the society, and the quality of this spirit is what determines the quality of the society.

Many people easily accept the idea of the spirit of a society, but they take it to be something subjective belonging to the people who make up the society. People say, "There's a good spirit in this society," and they talk about "team spirit" and imagine that they understand what is meant by these words or what is meant by a good or a bad spirit in a society. It is simply considered to be something that has to do with the state of mind of the people involved.

This does not account for the way in which societies behave. It is necessary to take it objectively, not just subjectively; there really is something that is not just the state of mind of people. The state of mind is just a partial manifestation of the spirit. If we come to something in which we share, it is not something that has to do with our states, which vary a great deal and greatly differ from person to person. It is a spirit that holds us together, as it is in any society that has a common aim, particularly when it is a spiritual aim.

The spirit of a society can persist in a most extraordinary way. About twenty years ago I visited Babylon for the first time. I was told that there was nothing much to see there because the Germans had taken away all the interesting finds in the 1890s and what was left was simply crumbling ruins worth only half an hour's visit. But when I got there, I found it totally different from what I had been told. I walked through the streets—they had been left exposed, which archaeologists today no longer do—and quite unmistakably I felt the spirit of the city. What I felt were not the individuals but the society of Babylon. One had become used to thinking of it as portrayed in the Hebrew scriptures, as a wicked city, but it was not at all like that. There was something very positive. In Babylon there was a very high and important culture, especially in the last period after the time of Cyrus.* Not all parts of the city felt the same. It is vast—thirty or forty miles long and about eight miles across, running right down to the Euphrates.

By contrast, on another occasion I went to Niniveh, the capital of the Assyrians. It is described in Zephaniah as already a desolation in the third or fourth century B.C. The city had been excavated but was basically a big mound. I felt the greatest antipathy toward the Assyrians, which I have never been able to get rid of. I felt the cruelty of the Assyrian empire as it was when Niniveh was built. It was a cruel and ruthless power, utterly different from the religious society of Babylon. That one could feel such things after two thousand or twenty-five hundred years was remarkable!

These experiences are possible because the spirit world is not subject to the same working of time as the material world: things can remain eternally as they are. It is possible to go back into the past and find a contact with the spirit reality that does not depend on the traces left behind.

We can look at societies in a similar way. A society is a pattern that interprets itself in action. The simplest society is that of the family. In natural human life this consists of three generations; it is only under artificial conditions that there are only one or two. Therefore a family is a manifestation of transmission. It must also be understood that a family has a certain reality of its own. It is not just a stage in the transmission from generation to generation. If it loses its special and unique character, then it is defective and deprives members of that family from contact with the spiritual world.

There are families where we can recognize a spirit—although its members may be quite different from each other in skills, powers, appearance, and so on—in which all participate. This kind of family is very necessary. People nowadays think that the family is only a temporary expedient providing conditions for children to be born and brought up. This is false.

The family has a natural extension in the clan or sept. In the family, the characteristic is that all members can know one another or place one another. In the sept, one may not know somebody directly,

*Founder of the Persian empire, died 529 B.C.

but one may know their parents and through this be connected with that person by thought and feeling. There is a very strong coherence in such a society.

People think that it does not matter that our modern civilization has disrupted this kind of society and replaced it by various kinds of artificial organizations for achieving results in the external world. It *does* matter: a certain spiritual reality is not allowed to come into being when there is that kind of disruption.

Beyond the range of awareness of the family, the clan, or the sept is the nation. The nation also has a spirit, and it is something very important and very difficult to destroy. This spirit is still largely a blood relationship and is the furthest this relationship reaches. Members of a nation are usually of the same race, and they do not have any sense of exogamy in marrying amongst themselves. They usually speak the same language, share in many customs, and form a geographical unit. Through such visible things the nation is recognizable, but the spirit of the nation is different from all that. This is easily seen in the case of the Jews, who lost all external forms of coherence in the Diaspora after the disasters of 70 A.D. but retained their national spirit. Similarly, the Kurds were ruthlessly broken up in Iraq, Iran, and what is now Persian territory, but there is unmistakably a Kurdish nation.

If one travels down the east side of Manhattan and into the Armenian district, one has exactly the same feeling as if one was in the Armenian district of Constantinople or Erzuroum. There is unmistakably an Armenian nation without there being any external form of unity.

Beyond the nation, we come to a society that expresses a common culture, united in ideas, feeling, and modes of behavior. This can go beyond the boundaries of nations and surpass the barriers of national antagonism. The word I use for this is *civilization,* a word I borrowed from Arnold Toynbee's *Study of History,* where he describes twenty or thirty different civilizations. The unity of a civilization is a unity of attitude toward life and a unity of values. It has to do with what people live for, and this comes out of the creative activity of relatively few people. Every civilization has its own independent source. This originally may be in people who are alien to the nation in which it arises, but it brings about a state of acceptance that allows people to trust one another because they have values that are right.

Civilization has never been universal. In the great land mass of Europe and Asia—also Africa—where there has been, geographically, perfect freedom of movement, there has never been one civilization that embraced all. Civilizations have risen and fallen, and while one declines in one area, another ascends in a different place. As the Greco-Roman civilization declined, the Arab civilization in Baghdad and Spain rose to prominence.

Again, the spirit of a civilization has a strange timeless character. This is very striking, for example, if one has traveled in Mexico. As one goes down from Mexico City to Oaxaca, Mitla, and Monte Alban, one comes into contact with a civilization that disappeared a millennium ago: the Zapotec. It is not like the sense of a place or region but of the values of that time. The Zapotec culture lasted about fifteen hundred years. Many people who have been in these regions are able to feel the way the people lived, what was important to them, what they would accept, and what they would reject.

It appears they had a tradition of destroying and rebuilding at certain intervals. They believed the world would come to an end at a certain time, and then they destroyed everything and went into the mountains. When the time passed, they returned and rebuilt. We have no conception of a culture that thinks it necessary to stop everything and start all over again with a fresh start. It would be wonderful if we could do such a thing every two or three hundred years. As a result of this practice, the Zapotecs had a singularly peaceful and harmonious existence—just because everything was temporary, and they had no need to hold on to things. They did turn into conquerors, but there is no evidence of civil wars.

Going one stage further than the civilization, we come to something that only a few historians like Toynbee, Spengler, and Giambattista Vico have tentatively suggested. It is connected with the idea of cycles and that there are large cycles that affect the whole of mankind, not just parts of it. There have been really major changes occurring every two or three thousand years. These periods of time I call *epochs*. An epoch is a period in human life when certain concepts of the sense and significance of human life predominate. We are now experiencing a change of epoch, the old one having ended perhaps a hundred years ago.

An epoch is pervaded by a master idea.[3] At the beginning of the last epoch, 500 B.C., new ideas about human life entered the world—from China and India to Central Asia, the near East, Europe, and even Central America. Confucius was contemporary with the Buddha and with the Jews after the Babylonian captivity. The new master idea brought about the state that recognized freedom and that was not based on slavery.

There are still greater periods of time. One of these began ten or twelve thousand years ago at the end of the Ice Age. Not only new ideas appeared but also fundamentally new societies, with new languages and ways of thinking. All the foundations of our modern world were laid then. The basic languages were created: the Indo-European or Aryan, the Hamitic from northeast Africa, and the agglutinative languages we associate with Tibet, China, and Turkestan. There were also formed corresponding religious beliefs: sun worship and the father-creator god of Egypt; the great universal spirit of Asia that went into China in the sophisticated form of Tao and was taken across by the migrations into America, where it appeared in the North American Indians; and the strange notion of the need for cooperation between the human and divine worlds that belonged to the Aryan peoples.[4] All of these tremendous creations came into being about twelve thousand years ago. We are probably now at the middle state of the great cycle that began at that time. Halfway through the cycle very great changes take place; it is like the change from spring to autumn.

If we go back a further twenty-five thousand years before the end of the Ice Age, we arrive at a time thirty-seven thousand years ago, when a new race of men appeared on the earth to replace Neanderthal man, who had dominated up until then. This new race was basically the same as our own race today. Very rapidly they took over the domination of the world and there were true men, of the Aurignacian culture, in the West and also as far east as the Caucasus.

Another race will be due to appear in twelve thousand years' time. They will have powers totally different from ours, just as the powers of Aurignacian man were totally different from those of Neanderthal man. The man who appeared about thirty-seven thousand years ago had a truly erect posture and the power of speech, which Neanderthal man was lacking. It requires a change in anatomy for man to be capable of articulating speech sounds, and previous to this, in all probability, language was very largely gestural. Sounds were used just to express emotions, not ideas. Gestures communicated what ideas there were. There is a theory that when speech came it was used first of all as a shorthand for gestures.

In looking at the history of human life, we can come to see that there is some kind of pattern that repeats itself, but in a different way each time. It is not a circle, but like spirals within spirals. The traces we have are the artifacts made by people, pictorial remains, and, much later, written records. By themselves, these traces would not allow us to see the pattern of the whole, but sometimes it is possible to grasp something of the spiritual side and see history "in the spirit."

This we need to do in order to grasp what is at work at the present time. There are two major transitions in progress: one is the change of epoch, and the other is the transition through the midpoint of a great cycle. Their coincidence means that the magnitude of events is much greater than in the previous changes of epoch.

Let us go back to the changes that came with the birth of the last major epoch, around 500 B.C. The world was profoundly affected by powerful ideas that were introduced by teachers such as Zoroaster, Buddha, Confucius, Lao Tzu, and the prophets of the captivity, particularly Isaiah. These ideas conveyed the sense of the sacredness of human life and the right of every individual to find his own salvation. This was quite revolutionary, totally alien to the previous epoch, where immortality was regarded as the prerogative of the very few: the priests, rulers, and heroes. Even where there were really beneficent rulers such as Hammurabi, the lawgiver of Mesopotamia, the feeling was that the ordinary people had nothing by right but only through the grace of the privileged few, who had direct contact with the gods. This led to enormous power being in the hands of the priesthood and rulers and made terrible tyrannies possible, such as that of the Assyrian kings. Inscriptions are still to be read of kings boasting of massacre and torture as a work of kingship. All that changed around 500 B.C. Of course, there have been tyrannies and there have been massacres since that time, but these are no longer regarded as human and even honorable but as inhuman and despicable.

Now we are coming to something quite new in human society. Human society completely changed twelve thousand years ago, with the beginning of settled communities and the creation of agriculture. We need to imagine something as profound as the change from a hunting and nomadic society to an agricultural and settled society. This is very difficult.

✧

IF THIS NEW WORLD is going
to be based on communities,
as I believe it will, the first
requirement is that people
shouldn't be slaves to their likes
and dislikes. If you can get rid of
that slavery, a community will
always work.

—From *Fallen Leaves*
A collection of J.G. Bennett's
writings, lectures, and letters.

Chapter 5

Psychokinetic Communities
Some Notes on Their Influence

THE MOST STRIKING EXAMPLE of psychokinetic influence took place in central Asia after the time of Ghengis Khan and lasted until the sixteenth century. In the thirteenth century in Khurasan, the Sufis gained a lot of influence by their practicality and their ability to communicate with people of different races and creeds. They undertook a lot of restorative work in the aftermath of the Mongol invasions. It was after the time of Tamerlane that the Sufis known as the Khwajagan came to a degree of organization that could be called a psychokinetic society.[1] At that point their actions became different. They began to influence public affairs to the point where, for two or three hundred years, Central Asia experienced an unprecedented period of relative peace, until the Russians took advantage of the conditions there and invaded and destroyed what had been built up.

The Khwajagan were able to exert an influence because they possessed, or were believed to possess, extraordinary powers. This is most clearly shown in the life and times of Ubaidallah Ahrar, the supreme master. For example, when Misa Khan was ruling in Samarkhand and Bokhara, his brother Ahmad tried to start an insurrection. Ahrar and his associates, through their control over energies, were able to produce such a portentous storm that the whole invading army was forced to flee, and the civil war was averted without any bloodshed.

There have been times when "religious" forces prevailed. Of particular interest is the early Persian empire of the Sassanids

51

(225–660 A.D.). The kings of this time, like Ardashir and the two Chosroes,* were largely submissive to the Zoroastrian teaching, though this period saw the establishment of Christianity, Manichaeanism, and the eventual rise of Islam. The question is whether there has been a time when the priestly caste as such could be said to have been a psychokinetic society. Manes (third century A.D.) was believed to have certain wonderful powers, and his followers did form a psychokinetic society that spread widely over the world at that time.

There was something in the Sassanid period that went back to the earlier time of the Achaemenids (fifth to third century B.C.), whose rule was finally broken by Alexander of Macedon. In *All and Everything,* Gurdjieff makes an enormous onslaught on Alexander, "this arch vain-glorious Greek" who destroyed the final traces of the labors of Ashiata Shiemash. His words precisely parallel those to be found in the later ninth century A.D. Pahlavi texts, which were intended to be faithful to what was contained in the early Zend Avesta of Achaemenid times. The ninth-century texts speak in great detail of Alexander's destruction of a hundred ox hides on which the original Zend Avesta, the Zoroastrian hymns and techniques, were written in gold ink. Gurdjieff turns this around and puts the account of the ox hides into his story of the *Kashireitleer* of Lentrohamsanin, the destroyer of Ashiata Shiemash's reforms.[2] This is a very striking confirmation of the idea that Ashiata Shiemash is intended to represent Zoroaster. It has always been very strange that although Gurdjieff could not have helped know-ing the importance of Zoroaster, he never once mentions his name. In all probability, the Magian power of the Sassanids had a great influ-ence on the Sufism of Central Asia, but we need to look at the events in the century after Zoroaster himself.

The overthrow of the Assyrian empire, which had lasted from the end of the second millennium, came through Cyrus. It was he who founded the Persian empire, liberated the Jews from captivity, and rebuilt the temple of Jerusalem. He was one of the great peacemakers of the world. After about a century, however, the whole thing had degenerated, and Cambyses appeared, who was nothing but a rather crazy conqueror. It is he who is described by Gurdjieff as bringing the wise men from Egypt to Babylon. The tradition concerning this is to be found in Iamblichus's *Life of Pythagoras,* which describes how Pythagoras went to Babylon and how Zoroaster was his teacher. It is an open question whether during that time (sixth century B.C.) the

*Named after the Achaemenid rulers Artaxerxes and Cyrus.

Zoroastrian brotherhood acted as a psychokinetic society with Babylon as its center.

In Tibet we had a very unusual situation of the psychokinetic society's gaining dominance and taking the wrong role. In the sixteenth and seventeenth centuries there was such an immense esteem paid to the monks that the balance between the psychostatic and the psychokinetic orders was disrupted. The lamas came to the point where they lived off the psychostatic population; they expected themselves to be supported and did not do any work themselves. A few schools maintained high standards, and there were two or three attempts at reform to restore the right balance. Gurdjieff's account in *All and Everything* describes events at the time of the Younghusband expedition into Tibet.

If we look at Christian Europe, one of the most remarkable changes in the working of the spiritual life took place with the rise of monasticism. Before then, monks had been concerned largely with withdrawal from the world and rejection of the world. They were in the tradition of the anchorites of the Egyptian and Syrian desert. A monk meant primarily one who had rejected the world. We can discern their attitude in the institutes of Cassian. There were tens of thousands of monks and nuns, some of them living the solitary life and others, the Kenobitic monks, living together. Those who worked out a way of living together flourished in Syria, from which came the Carmelite order, and in the Libyan desert at the border of Egypt. These spiritual men and women worked in this way from the third to the seventh century. Then came the Gothic invasions, the collapse of the Roman Empire, and the lapse of Roman influence. Thereafter, the role of the monks greatly changed.

The rule of Saint Benedict is essentially different from the rules of the monks of the desert, such as those of Cassian. In the monasteries of the desert, the problem of the denying force was in relationships between monks and in the relationship with the physical body. But when the world came into disarray, then the world itself was the embodiment of the denying force. The idea was brought forward of the obligation to serve the world and not to turn away from the world. The rule of Saint Benedict puts forward the obligation to care for people, first of all through hospitality and then through service to the surrounding community. This is the kind of thing that becomes important when the psychokinetic order is confronted with a need in the world.

The Benedictine monks, or the other orders that arose from the

influence of the rule, were concerned with the re-establishment of agriculture, preserving herds and flocks of sheep, and providing seed
crops. They also took on the work of education, because the schools
provided through the Romans largely collapsed.

Just as later the Sufis in Central Asia converted the invaders to
Islam, so the monks converted the Goths to Christianity. The monks
also fell into the trap that later the lamas in Tibet fell into: they began
to live off the psychostatic community. This led to all the abuses that
eventually led to the Reformation and the dissolution of the
monasteries.

We can also look at the Ottoman empire, particularly in the fifteenth century. Right up to the collapse of Constantinople in 1453,
they were very much influenced by Sufi societies. When the Seljuk
empire broke down, social order from Persia to the Mediterranean
broke down. Then the Bektashis[3] played much the same role as the
Christian monks in Europe. They were intimately involved with the
welfare of the people, especially in education. From the Bektashis
came the Janissaries, the most powerful influence in the army, who
had a great influence on the rulers.

The rulers had advisers not only in the religious sense but also
through the specialist craftsmen they had brought from Samarkhand.
The ceramics of the age were superb—as at Bursa—and this had a
great influence on the people. Many of the rulers were artists and
musicians rather than administrators. There were also great physicians. There were certain dervish orders who largely gave their services through medicine.

The whole of this established a right kind of relationship between
those who entered the order and devoted themselves to self-perfecting
and those who belonged to the psychostatic order.

In the early Christian church there was no evidence of any positive
involvement in the world, especially if we look at the churches founded
by Saint Paul and his admonitions to them. They regarded themselves
as separate from the world, and their powers were to be used only for
the good of their own community, the charismata. They had no expectation of exerting an influence on the world because they thought that
the end of the world would come before anything like that could
happen.

Power over nature—power in the ordinary sense—is not the prerogative of the psychokinetic society. The people who have discovered
how to double the production of food crops in India, how to release
atomic energy, or how to travel with great speed and convenience

have done so from a psychostatic attitude and for psychostatic pur-
poses, for aims within the material world. A psychokinetic society
cannot compete with this, except possibly in the field of medicine. It
may be that psychostatic medicine is failing because medicine comes
too close to the real problem of man, which is the fulfillment of his
destiny.

Gurdjieff in *Beelzebub's Tales* refers to the physicians, the *zirlik-
ners,* as the leaders of the psychokinetic society. It may be that healing
could be developed in a psychokinetic society in such a way that it
would exert a really powerful influence on people of the psychostatic
order. There are examples of this in the lives of saints like Catherine
of Genoa, who with her nuns nursed the people at a time of plague.
For the most part, they themselves appeared to be immune and did
not get infected when everybody around them did, and this made a
profound impression.

Very possibly, an important role could be taken by a psychokinetic
society today in the realm of natural medicine. There is something
essentially artificial in the present medical system, which is based
mainly on chemotherapy and which uses substances that have a powerful action on the human organism. This system seems to be as
wrong as our educational system, which is essentially psychostatic in
outlook, and our economic system, which is directly hostile to the psychokinetic ideal because it depends largely on keeping people as they
are: good domestic animals.

✧

THE POSSIBILITY of realizing our destiny depends upon a force that is not our own and that has its origin on a much higher level than the human. Therefore, everything for us really depends upon the possibility of coming into contact with that great force.

—From *Fallen Leaves*
A collection of J.G. Bennett's writings, lectures, and letters.

Chapter 6

The Sermon on the Mount

Part 1

THE GOSPELS WERE WRITTEN for Christians living at the end of the first century, still remembering the persecutions of Nero (54–68 A.D.) and the tremendous catastrophe of the destruction of Jerusalem by Titus (70 A.D.). The reign of terror under Domitian was at its height, and yet the Christians were already aware that they had a great destiny to fulfill in the world. The Sermon on the Mount consists partly of authentic sayings of Jesus recorded in two or three long-lost manuscripts and partly of extracts from the Old Testament used by the author, or group of authors, to amplify some of the precepts. As we can see by comparing the gospel of Matthew with that of Mark, the material was rearranged, amplified, and carefully structured to produce a practical manual rather than a record of teaching.[1]

We should look upon the Sermon as a training manual for Christians who were preparing themselves for the task of providing the world with a way of life that would survive the coming collapse of the human civilization. Not many could see so far ahead, and those who did so were inspired by the higher powers. The Sermon on the Mount is remarkable not only in itself but also in its timing. Its message was alien to all contemporary thought—Jewish, Greek, Roman, and Oriental—and it was even very different from the message of Saint Paul in his Epistles and from that of the Acts of the Apostles and the beliefs of the early Christians before 70 A.D., who were expecting the "second coming" of Christ in the early future.

For us, in the last decades of the twentieth century, the Sermon on the Mount has a new significance, because we are witnessing similar upheavals and we also know that we have to prepare for a great destiny that lies ahead. The concepts on which the greatness of European culture was built are losing their validity, just as those on which the greatness of Greece and Rome were founded were losing

57

theirs at the time when the Sermon on the Mount was compiled. Just as Rome under Vespasian and Trajan during the last three decades of the first century was at the height of its glory and appeared capable of maintaining a *pax Romana* throughout the world, so now we see the overwhelming dominance of modern technology and a blind confidence in its power to establish a universal *pax technica,* without renewal of its ethic. Herein lies the basic error of our time and of theirs.

Those who have seen that there can be no progress without a new ethic—and they exist in every part of the world—have the task of preparing for the future. Many see the need but do not know how it is to be met. Those who see that this can come only and exclusively by a transformation of the inner life are in the same position as the Christians of the Diaspora, the dispersal after the destruction of Jerusalem in 70 A.D. We, too, have had our diaspora, which was the consequence of the two world wars and which shattered the illusion of permanent European hegemony. We know that something entirely new and different must come, but we are not yet ready to receive it. This is the context of our work.

If we turn again to the Sermon on the Mount, we should first notice the paradoxical and unpredictable character of the new ethic. The Beatitudes reverse ordinary notions of blessedness. If we remember that the Greek word for blessed, *makarios,* was applied to the gods of Olympus, we can see how very paradoxical the Beatitudes must have appeared to the Greeks and Romans who first heard them. No less a shock to the Jews was contained in the six "renewals" of the old law that complete chapter 5 [of Saint Matthew's gospel].

These renewals are not commandments in the Jewish sense, nor are they philosophical principles in the Greek sense. They are practical counsels of self-perfecting that indicated the way in which those preparing for the new age were to look at their relationships to the world about them. The whole of chapter 5 can be taken as an instrument of self-examination. We can compare our behavior and our disposition, point by point, with those expressed in the seven sections of the chapter—the Beatitudes and the six perfections—and we can ask ourselves not only how we stand but how we wish to stand. "Would I wish, if I were able, to live according to these standards of disposition and conduct?" This question is intensely practical for us now, since we have to put analogous, though different, questions to ourselves.

The second point to be noted are the obvious contradictions that require the Christian to be fully in the world and yet fully apart from it at the same time. He must let his light shine before men [5.3-16] and yet hide his good deeds [6.1-15]. He is to give to him that asketh [5.42], even if he is evil and unjust [5.45], and yet he is not to give what is holy to the dogs [7.6]. He is not to judge [7.1], and yet he must be able to recognize the unworthy seeker and refrain from casting his pearls before swine [7.6]. All these apparent contradictions show that the Christian is not to rely upon the letter of the law or look for instructions to relieve him of his own decisions. He must understand the principles of Christian action, and he must do so by action rather than by thought [6.27, 7.13, and 7.24–27]. The final exhortation [7.24–27] gives the key to the whole matter: *the Sermon is a practical document concerned with doing.*

Christian beliefs are taken for granted; the aim is to work for the kingdom of God [6.33] and to do so in full reliance that all that is necessary will be provided [6.25-34]. The world is threatened with destruction, but there is a "straight gate" that leads to life [7.13], and the disciples are invited to choose this way, forewarned of the demands it will make upon them.

There is no suggestion of a set of commandments. The old law is not set aside, but it is to be understood in a new way [5.17-20]. The inner attitude is no less important than the outward conduct: both are needed. Under the old law, conduct alone counted. The Oriental cults that were gaining popularity all through the Roman Empire placed all the emphasis in ecstasy and mystical experience. They tried to invade Christianity by way of Gnosticism, and the New Testament books compiled at the end of the first century have many warnings against reliance on "spirits." The Sermon on the Mount avoids equally the pitfalls of literalism and of illuminism.[2] It does this by a special means that must be not only thought about but practiced if it is to be understood. Nothing is precisely explained or enjoined; hints only are given as to the way the disciples were to be "in the world but not of it." The Sufis refer to this as *halwat dar anjuman,* or solitude among the crowd.

For us, the lesson is that if we are to take our part in the spiritual undertaking that is now in progress, we also must learn to live in more than one world at the same time. We cannot separate the inner and the outer worlds effectively and safely unless we strengthen the "third world" in ourselves. The Sermon on the Mount contains implicitly the same idea. It is directed, through and through, to the interaction between the higher and lower parts of man's nature and between the spiritual and the material levels of being, between man and God.

At first glance, the demands made upon us seem to be beyond our power. If we put away this first reaction and take them one by one, we can ask ourselves, "Is this really impossible for me? Could I not set myself to live according to this particular precept?" We shall then find that it is a matter of decision. All that is proposed in the Sermon is possible for us if we choose to do it. We are hampered by our lack of self-confidence and our fear of the world. We can remind ourselves that nothing can touch our "I" and that if we are even a little conscious we are stronger than the "world."

The last question that is raised by the Sermon is "Why should we live this way? Were not these precepts spoken and written for people under totally different conditions of life?" This is true, and the Sermon on the Mount is not to be taken literally. But this does not mean that we can allow ourselves lower standards. The demands made on us if we are to serve the Work today are different, but they are not less. The advantage to us of studying the Sermon on the Mount is that it gives us the opportunity of putting ourselves in the position of other people faced with a world crisis like our own and offered the opportunity of helping "from within." It was a training manual, but it was certainly not used in private. There were teachers, and there were groups whose influence was at first scarcely noticed but who were connected with the amazing impact of Christianity on the Roman world that began to gain momentum in the second century. We, too, must not forget that though our work is invisible to the contemporary world, its fruits will appear in their season.

✧

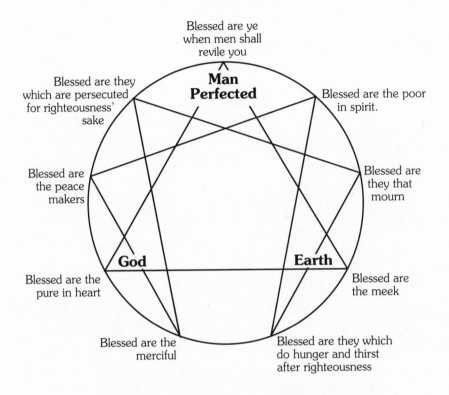

Blessed are ye when men shall revile you

Man Perfected

Blessed are they which are persecuted for righteousness' sake

Blessed are the poor in spirit.

Blessed are the peace makers

Blessed are they that mourn

God

Earth

Blessed are the pure in heart

Blessed are the meek

Blessed are the merciful

Blessed are they which do hunger and thirst after righteousness

The Enneagram of the Beatitudes

The enneagram is a symbol of self-sustained transformation. This symbolic device originated, according to Gurdjieff, with the Sarmaun Brotherhood, twenty-five hundred years ago in Central Asia. For more information on the enneagram, the reader is referred to J.G. Bennett, *Enneagram Studies* (*see* Bibliography).

Part 2

THE FIRST THING THAT IS SAID in the Sermon on the Mount is that a separation took place. There was the multitude and there were the disciples, and in order to separate, the disciples had to climb up into a mountain. This represents the difference in level between life and the Work. The Sermon on the Mount is certainly addressed to people who wish to "work." Many times in this Gospel Jesus says, "I speak to you in one way; I speak to them another way. I tell you plainly about the kingdom of heaven, and I tell the people in general by means of parables, indirectly." Here he was dealing only with the disciples, and he spoke to them directly. The picture has to be in our minds that the Sermon is addressed to people who work, who have the intention to work. And clearly, if it is addressed to those people, it is intended to be accepted and acted upon by them, which is emphasized by the final passage, in which he says, "He who hears these words of mine and does them, it is like building a house on a rock." So, as clearly as possible it is stated that the Sermon on the Mount is a practical document intended to be taken as a way of life by those people who were disciples.

If we ourselves wish to work, we must ask ourselves whether this document, or perhaps a modern equivalent of it, represents for us a way of life. Only a small part of the Sermon on the Mount, the Beatitudes, is concerned with the inner life, with inner-world demands [see illustration page 61]. Why are they put at the beginning? Because they represent the test, the conditions. If you will accept these as what you are committed to, then read on—then the rest of this applies to you. Otherwise not. If this corresponds to your inner state now—or if you have got the seed of the possibility of being like this—then what I am going to say applies to you.

The first and last of the nine Beatitudes refer to the conditions for what Christ calls the kingdom of heaven, and the whole of this chapter is concerned with the kingdom of heaven. What does the kingdom of heaven mean? He does not say the kingdom *in* heaven or the kingdom in some other world. The kingdom of heaven is clearly a state of affairs in this world. He begins by saying, "Blessed are the poor in spirit: for theirs is the kingdom of heaven," which means "Blessed are those who have seen their own nothingness," those who are empty. They are the people who are able to enter.

To arrive at the point of seeing one is nothing requires a lot of preparatory work, all of which is presupposed, just as the disciples go up to the mountain and the whole exposition does not begin until they have climbed the mountain. The first indication of having climbed the mountain is to recognize one's own nothingness; from that point everything can begin. So long as one is burdened by the illusion of having something—having something to protect, having some spiritual wealth, one cannot begin. He makes it clear that he is not talking about poverty in the material sense but in the spiritual sense: one does not have anything of one's own, one has no "I," one is not awake. This realization represents the threshold of this work of ours. The starting point for everyone coming to this work is the realization that we have no spiritual possessions. This brings the awareness of being separated, which is represented by "mourning": "Blessed are they that mourn."

When we bring our attention to the wish that comes from the sense of separation and the need to find our source again, this leads on to hope: "for they shall be comforted." In Greek it is very beautiful. It was probably written in Greek, and therefore Greek is the language in which to understand it. *Makarioi hoi penthoontes, hoti owtoi para-klaythaysonteye*.[3] The next Beatitude is translated "Blessed are the meek: for they shall inherit the earth." This is the key to understanding everything that is going to come afterward. A new world is to be built. The Sermon on the Mount is about a new world, about leaving behind the old world and building a new world on gentleness.

Each one of the Beatitudes gradually unfolds the picture of the kind of state that must be reached in order to enter the kingdom of heaven.

I said before that it is only the early verses that refer to the inner state. From then onward it is very noticeable that almost everything is about the way we live. It is a document that refers to a community, how people will live together in this new world. There is very little in the Sermon on the Mount that is about our private lives; nearly everything is about our lives within a community. This community will have to suffer because it is going to be a stranger in the world. This is made clear many times. It is finally put in quite specific terms: "Blessed are ye when men shall revile you and persecute you and shall say all manner of evil against you falsely, for my sake." Such is inevitable, because this community is to be a stranger in the world, and its ways are not the ways of the world. But this has happened before, and you are not to be dismayed by this because it has happened whenever there have been people chosen for a special task as the prophets were. Whenever people were called upon to perform spiritual tasks in the world, the world never accepted them. It is what is said here and, of course, said many times all through the rest of the Gospel. "So persecuted they the prophets that were before you." That is the attitude with which you should come.

Be prepared to give: "Blessed are the merciful."

Then, of course, the big thing, the hard thing, comes: to be pure in heart. This really goes beyond knowing one's inner emptiness, which is in the first Beatitude. It is when this emptiness has been accepted and there is no longer a striving to fill oneself with things, when one consciously makes oneself nothing. Then comes the time when the "third force," the reconciling force, can work: "Blessed are they who construct peace, who make peace." The making of peace is the work of the third force. That is why they are called "children of God," because God is the third force, which now has been born in them. But they will have to suffer, so it comes back again to "Blessed are they that are persecuted for righteousness' sake" and so on. In the first and last, the kingdom of heaven comes in.

If you really meditate on the Beatitudes, you see that collectively they represent an attitude that allows the person who is like that to be filled with the divine working. Why is all this? What is it all for? Because they have to manifest. So there follow at once references to the "salt of the earth" and the "light of the world." There is the manifestation that is required. That is stated clearly at the beginning. All sorts of things will have to happen in order to make this possible, but this is what you are here for. If you have not got this right, then whatever else you may think of, you are good for nothing: you should be cast out and trodden under the foot of men. You have to have that flavor, you have to have that taste of salt about you, you have to have that light showing from you; people have to recognize through you the working of the third force.

Then how is this new world to come about? Is it to come about by destroying all the old institutions, killing off the dinosaurs? No, they will be left—all this has got to work itself out and will work itself out. There is no need to concern oneself with the old institutions; all that has got to work itself out and be finished with. Something new has to arise. That this is something new is said all through the rest of this chapter: "It has been said by them of old time" that the old world was like that and the new world has got to be a different kind of world—not a world of cause and effect, not a world where things are bought and sold.

You have got to have this kind of standard in your community: that you are going to live differently and your relationships are going to be of a different kind. All the rest of the chapter is about the transformation of relationships that belongs to the new community. In the old world was the principle of not killing, but here you replace it by a principle of acceptance. Accept your brother; make peace with him. It is not sufficient to abstain from harming; it is necessary to discover a positive attitude. Simply keeping rules of not harming and killing and judging, and so on, is not enough. Your community will not hold together on the basis of rules; it has got to be on the basis of an attitude.

I have spoken before of one interpretation of "If thine eye offend thee, pluck it out." When I spoke about "chief feature,"[4] I said that this is a cause of offense to us and to others, but it is not by destroying it but by an act of separation or not identifying that we liberate ourselves. We have to be able to look with an eye that does not offend; we have to be able to act with hands that will not offend.

The relationship between men and women has to be different in this community; they have to see that it is not an external relationship in time, which can change in time like everything in time does change, but a different kind of relationship. They must always look for this "other quality" in life but not by means of rules, contracts, and the rest of it.

The new way goes much further, much deeper than anything before, by not resisting evil nor even trying to put things right. This could not be understood except in the search for an ideal community. To allow oneself to be imposed on is the secret of a community that can withstand pressures and be transformed: no one to insist upon his rights or her rights but to allow themselves to be imposed on or to be made a fool of. This has to be learned as a way of life. This is one of the things where it begins to look very hard. People will say, "But how can we do this? If we always give way, where will it all end? We shall be just trampled on, made into slaves." "Yes," Jesus says, "that is true enough about the world, but not in this community, not here."

This way of life has only one rule: the rule of perfection. Everything else is insufficient for it. He finishes with "Be ye therefore perfect, even as your Father which is in heaven is perfect." Who is the "Father in heaven?" Where is this "heaven?" Certainly the disciples perfectly well understood that heaven was not a place somewhere; they perfectly well understood that in every one of us there is heaven. And there is a heaven that we share, only we shut ourselves out from it.

The Father is ourselves, that part of us that is in the unconditioned world; from that we have come. We must mould our lives according to the pattern, the dharma, of our real being—obey and accept our dharma.

The whole of this chapter consists just of illustrations of the way in which we will be required to live if our community is to work. What were such communities? At that time, there were many communities that were being formed not only by Christians but others also. There were Mithraic communities, and there were communities of the old gods. But the Christian communities were setting themselves a certain task; they were all standing before the prophecy of the end of the world. They were expecting the old world to die and the new world to come, and they were to prepare themselves for that. Some communities, particularly the ones in Syria, misunderstood this because they thought that one should abandon all interest in life. They were being told that you must not marry, there must be no relations between men and women, you must abandon everything, because none of this has any relevance for the world that is to come. But nowhere for those for whom this document, this *legominism*, was constructed, is there suggested that one should not marry and continue one's normal life and fulfill all one's outward obligations. Only they were to get a certain strength that could come only by their own way of life—their own communal way of life—so that they would be able to withstand.

Of course, the strains and stresses did come. The communities were persecuted, and many people were martyred. An extraordinary strength was shown all through the second century, when without it the seed would have died. You must understand that this was a very farseeing preparation for a time of trouble that was coming. Without setting themselves these high standards of work on themselves and of acceptance of one another, they could not have withstood it, not only because they would not have had the support of one another but, what is more important, because they would not have had the necessary energy.

It happened very often that these communities escaped being destroyed and annihilated, against all odds. For the most part, these were in the Jewish communities of the Diaspora, the dispersion after the destruction of Jerusalem in 70 A.D. There was a great congregation in Alexandria and on the coast of Egypt. Jerusalem had been virtually wiped out at this time. For the most part, the Jews returned to a very strict way of life. They took refuge in the law [of Moses]. When the temple was destroyed, the law became their temple. They maintained a very high standard of life, and they were also constantly persecuted and in danger. Their way was to go for a very strict observation of the law and preservation of everything that belonged to their life. This also preserved them, and they survived this time of trouble, but their role was different. The communities following the Sermon on the Mount were after something different from rigid observances.

Within the community, those who *have* must give and work for those who lack. Therefore, the first thing that has to be looked at is, how does this giving and taking come about? There is the law of alms giving: you have to give a proportion of your possessions to help the poor, by the sacred law. But in what way? This is not a thing to be seen by people; this is not where you are to be a light—a different manifestation from that is required. Therefore, it is not to be done in this way, to be seen by people. At first it looks as if there is obviously a great contradiction between the saying "Let your light so shine before men that they shall see your good works" and "See that you do not give your alms before men, to be seen of them." Anyone can notice this contradiction and many other contradictions. How this light is to shine is not through these visible actions, not by observance of laws and customs, but by what it is that emanates, what it is that this community has in itself. This is the secret part of the Work. Very simple rules are now beginning to come in—or, rather, principles are being explained, not rules of conduct.

For example, there is the principle of the two stages of work. When someone makes some kind of work effort or work sacrifice, the reward for this is to be put in front of some temptation, which means the possibility of doing something different. In this case, the temptation is to be appreciated for having given alms. The real work here is not really in giving but in not expecting to be thanked for it. That is where freedom lies: to give in such a way that one will not be thanked or appreciated for giving. Learn that secret, and then you will have made a connection with the Father, with the inner world, the inner being. This also applies to the other examples given about praying and fasting.

The second chapter of the Sermon on the Mount is throughout concerned with how to reach the kingdom of heaven, how to become such a community. These are the secrets, the methods, that you have to be ready to use. Hide your work as much as possible to contain the energy that comes from one's efforts, from one's sacrifices; do not feed on it but allow it to accumulate and build up. Then it begins to be shared, and other people begin to participate in it; then it is that we are able to do something, really, to help other people. This action is described at the end of the Lord's Prayer: "Forgive us as we forgive each other."

To talk about the Lord's Prayer in detail is a big thing, but I will say a few things about it. The first thing one has to ask oneself is what is meant by "vain repetitions" as used by the heathens. This sounds as if it was just a kind of rejection of the Mithraic cult, which used a great deal of mantrams. What is a vain repetition? Vain really means empty of substance. There has to be an actual material substance of prayer: it is made of something.

There is also the question of what is meant by Father. Why *our* Father? Why not *my* Father? The prayer is a communal prayer; there is no *I* in it, no first person. It is always *our* Father, *our* trespasses, *our* daily bread. It is a prayer for a community. But what is "Father" in this? What does it mean? It means that this world in which we are living has its origin in another world. One must never think that this is the original world, that this is where it starts. It is not so—it all comes from another world. This is why it is said, "Which art in heaven"—not here, because this is not where it starts. It starts on the unconditioned side.

As it is said by one of the Apostles later on—about the same time the Sermon was written—"Every good gift comes from above, from the Father of Light." It comes out of the unconditioned world, which our knowledge cannot reach, which we cannot penetrate and have direct experience of; therefore we make this acknowledgement. It is why we speak not of God but of the Father, and not of the Father but of the name ["Hallowed be thy name"]. We cannot go beyond the name, or the image. We do not know what is behind this image. This is really the first thing that is made clear here: where we are called to, where we come from, is beyond this world of body and mind. We have not access to it; we can only believe that it is there. It is presented to us only as an image. All sacred images are only images of the name that we are blessing. But then, how is it that we ask that the kingdom should come? Because the kingdom has to come into this world; it has to appear and establish itself here in this world. This is what is said clearly here and elsewhere. That was the teaching; that is what they were taught, how they were taught to look at it. There is the pattern, the dharma, in heaven—on the other side. But it is to be accomplished here—"Thy will be done in Earth"—here in this conditioned world.

Many people have questioned what is meant by "daily bread." It has been translated in different ways from the Greek, sometimes using words that mean the higher bread, the supersubstantial bread. It does not matter. Some way or another we need food, all kinds of food. But some food comes to us from the unconditioned world, which is the food that we cannot collect for ourselves, that we cannot prepare, that has to be given to us.

Then there is this notion of acceptance of one another, forgiveness of one another, which we put down as the condition for the possibility of our being related to the other world; as long as there is rejection, as long as we reject others, we are rejecting the way to the other world. The same prayer appears elsewhere, but there it is underlined by repeating over again, "If you don't forgive you will not be forgiven." Let that be clear, because you cannot have the community you are looking for on the basis of demands made upon one another.

If you study this middle chapter of the Sermon on the Mount, you see that it is all about the relation between the conditioned and the unconditioned worlds. It says so in almost so many words: "Don't lay up for yourselves treasures on earth, but in heaven." Earth always represents the conditioned world, heaven always the unconditioned world— the two sides of our nature. Everything is about how this divorce between the two sides of our nature is to be healed.

Then comes something that is very relevant for us, and one really has to ponder on this a great deal. In the rest of this chapter are many references to "not taking thought," not planning. He says there are two ways of living, in effect. One way of living is to trust the pattern, to trust the dharma. The other way of living is to trust your own capacity for calculating. If you choose to calculate, then you put yourself under the laws of this earth. If you are prepared not to calculate but to trust the laws of dharma, the pattern of things, this will then take care of you. This is the kind of community you have to form: a community that is based upon trust in the pattern, trust in the dharma. Absurd as it is, can you by any calculation add an inch to your height? Can't you see the limits of human calculation? This is how the world is trying to run: it is trying to run on calculation, on planning and preparation, on confidence in the working of natural laws and with quantitative knowledge to adapt the world to your liking, to gain control over it. The advice is perfectly clear: that is not how the community is to work. It is to work on the basis of confidence in the dharma, in the pattern.

All these illustrative details show how much importance is attached to this, as in the first chapter so much importance is attached to the emphasis on "this community is a new one." It is not to be based on the same principles as those before. Here Jesus says it again: it is not only that it is a new community, but it has got a different principle of living. It is to live by the heavenly eye, the heavenly ear—the discernment of the pattern of things, seeing rather than calculating, allowing oneself to be led by trusting . . . those kinds of things.

The last chapter comes to the actual relations between the members of the community. First, not judging, and then there comes "Whatever you would men should do to you, you do that to them"—simple principles of relationship in the kind of community that is to be set up. It is never said, but it is implied, that it is not a hierarchical community; there is no head to it because it works as one whole.

I have given you an idea that for me is very important: that one should see that the Sermon on the Mount is a document containing some very important principles of living—methods of achieving a community that has its own inner life, that is not subject to disruptive forces. This is not generally emphasized in commentaries on the Sermon on the Mount; possibly it is taken for granted—I do not know. But, of course, the Sermon on the Mount sets a very high standard of living. It must be looked at as something that was put in front of real people, men and women who were living under certain conditions. These were not unlike our conditions, and that is why it is important for us to know about it. The one difference is that it was relatively local. The collapse of all the institutions on which people depended applied almost only to the Roman Empire. And now it is worldwide. We have to look forward to the need to be able to live in a world that will be very unfavorable, and if we are not prepared to set ourselves these standards, or at least equivalent standards, then it will not be so easy to survive.

I think it is obvious that this is all about a community. One reason, perhaps, why people overlook this point and that it is not noticed is that it is not based, as it is with us, on having some kind of hierarchy, some people with authority over other people. One can see that this concerns a community without power and without authority. At the same time, it is a community that is expected to perform a service in the world, because Jesus says at the beginning, "Your light must shine, you must be a beacon, you must be a 'lighthouse'—something to show people the way to safety."

Anyhow, here are suggestions for looking at the Sermon on the

Mount. For me, it has been for many, many years a document that I have lived with. I have always asked myself, "Can you live according to that?" Is there anything here that can make me say, "I cannot do that, this is not possible for me"? More and more I have come to see that it is not so, that at no point whatever have I found anything that is written in the Sermon on the Mount that could make me say that this is something I cannot do—that if I did this, things would go wrong. It is the very contrary.

Supposing one were to contemplate a community that really took from beginning to end the Sermon on the Mount as the principle of the way of living. Then people would be together, people would not be trampled on, people would not be taken advantage of. There would be very great strength in such a community and very great happiness. There was very great happiness in these early communities that were based on these principles.

✦

Chapter 7

Characteristics of the Psychokinetic Life

WE SHOULD BE ABLE TO SPEAK OF LOVE without fear of mixing it with our own self. We need to be able to recognize the state in us when we are able to love. What is needed are certain basic skills connected with "letting go." We need to be able to let go of possessions and physical things, and we need also to be free emotionally so that we are not attached. If we find ourselves not in the required state, we must be able to bring ourselves inwardly into a state of letting go.

There is a letting go required to remove a certain obstacle so that love can arise spontaneously toward someone we do not feel sympathy with. This we should constantly practice. One can dislike but also love. Love is from the will, and it is an act of will and is unconnected with attraction or aversion. The secret of working with love from oneself is in the saying of Jesus "Love thine enemy." This we can work at when we have "againstments," bringing the feeling of love, which has to be impartial, into our minds and trying to have this toward the person we are "against." We can see that it is possible to love that person.

It is not easy to love people we like. With them, the whole thing is to be free of expectations. With people we dislike, it is easier. With those we care about, there are demands and attachments, which are our ego, not love. It is possible to open ourselves more and more to people with whom there are againstments. Whatever is right is always possible.

If we worked without authority, we would first of all have to recognize that there would be negative behavior, and we would have to accept this. Where does the element that is contrary to the Work enter? This we must really understand. The Work consists in recognizing that our nature is what it is. This means that we accept the denying force in ourselves, but with the implication of the words "holy denying."[1]

There is the question of roles. These are needed. People may be

72

elected to them, or they may be rotated. There also may be specialist roles. Is it desirable to think in terms of maximum interchangeability of roles? Is it desirable to avoid specialization except for efficiency?

These questions are important, but there is a more important one. Could we accept one another and face how we are? We know we are all rather different. We can make different contributions. But, more seriously, nobody in the psychokinetic group is perfect. Our imperfections touch on other people's lives. We begin to see that it is possible to tolerate and accept what people do but there remains an undercurrent of feeling. Underneath there is "So and so does this. So and so does that." This is something very crucial. Can we look at it?

What is needed is to put society first and ourselves second. We need therefore to be able to accept the differences between people—some contribute more, some less—that have a disruptive effect. The usual attitude of people in society is based on right and wrong. This belongs to the "cataclysm not according to law," when the reality of human life was lost to mankind."[2]

What is needed is to change our attitude entirely toward the denying force. The denying force is the only point of return to the source. This is the origin of the action that matters. It is not a question of somebody being in need of help, because in reality we all have the problem of the denying force. In a real psychokinetic community, everyone realizes that everyone presents toward the others a denying force.

There is the question of decision making. Is this to be by consensus, authority, or discussion? Or is there something different from both democracy and autocracy? Groups like the Society of Friends wait together for guidance. What we are after is that everyone should share in a vision of the situation. In simple practical work, it is possible to work in this way without supervisors and instructors. Can this be extended?

This belongs to the ultimate criterion expressed by Gurdjieff in the phrase "Only he may enter here who is able to put himself in the place of the other results of my labors."[3] In living together, one has to play a role. One must know and judge—"external considering"—but be free inside so that one does not manifest exactly as one feels. This is the middle way. Only when one can put oneself in the place of another should one say things to them that may enter them deeply.

The denying force is the condition of affirmation. Until this is understood fully there cannot be an objective life.

✧

MAN DIDN'T COME into this
world for nothing. Man is an
extraordinary achievement that has
required long and difficult preparation.
This achievement is not complete.
It would be quite a considerable cosmic
disaster if this experiment with man on
this earth were to fail, and for this reason
much is being done to prevent this
experiment from failing—not because
man deserves to survive, but because
he is really needed.

Appendix A

The Fourth Way

J.G. Bennett's last public talk: November 6th, 1974,
Friend's House, London. It has been slightly edited for publication.

WE CALL THIS LECTURE "Gurdjieff's Fourth Way" because he introduced this term in the West, but the idea is very much older. To my knowledge it goes back about eight hundred or nine hundred years, to a time not unlike the present. The idea is this: There are times when the world goes through a crisis—the way of life to which people have been accustomed is threatened—and there is bewilderment; at such times people look for guidance and reassurance so that they can retain a worthwhile life during all the changes that are happening.

I said that this idea of a "fourth way" goes back a long time. The first reference to it that I know is about twenty-five hundred years ago in the time of Zoroaster, when the agricultural communities of Central Asia were threatened by the nomads and the Turanians from the north; at that time there was a great conflict that lasted a long time between the nomadic tribes and the settled populations. One of the main elements of Zoroaster's teaching was that we must preserve the earth, we must preserve agriculture, and that there is a duty of service that is the core of religion—and this *duty* is the core of the Zoroastrian religion.

Later, when to my knowledge the term was actually introduced as the Fourth Way, there was a great teacher of the twelfth century, Abd al-Khaliq Ghujduwani* from Bokhara in Central Asia. At that time there was peace and great prosperity there. Samarkhand and Bokhara had become great centers of learning and culture. But there was also a threat that people refused to recognize, a threat of devastation from the north that did in fact occur about seventy or eighty years later. Abd

---

*For more information about Abd al-Khaliq Ghujduwani and other "masters of wisdom" the reader is referred to J.G. Bennett, *The Masters of Wisdom* (London: Turnstone Press, 1980).

75

al-Khaliq spoke of it in this way: We have to find our way of spiritual perfecting. Some find it through the "intellectual way," and there is this great intellectual culture that surrounds us, and it is a good thing. Others find it by the "way of devotion" and particularly the devotion to a teacher (which became a very strong cult at that time, as it was also in India), and this way of devotion and love is also good. There is also the "way of withdrawal" from the world—particularly the ascetic withdrawal—and of that he said that solitude is dangerous. Withdrawal is a way to become famous and fame is disastrous, and we must avoid that. We have to go by a "fourth way," and I think that's when the term was first used, and this fourth way must be the way of service and the way of shared effort.

Abd al-Khaliq Ghujduwani was, I think, the one who founded the notion of working in groups under the lead of a teacher. I won't go into the details of it, but the point is this: When Abd al-Khaliq was instituting this Fourth Way, people refused to believe that the way of life to which they were accustomed was threatened—even though they could see the growing menace of the Tartar.

Then, at the beginning of the thirteenth century, Genghis Khan appeared—the greatest conqueror perhaps who has ever lived. He created the Mongol nation just about the time that Abd al-Khaliq Ghujduwani was saying all this, and in 1220 he conquered Bokhara and Samarkhand. Hundreds of thousands of people were killed; probably, in the aggregate, several million people were killed. The cities were devastated. The irrigation system that had made this one of the most prosperous parts of the world—an irrigation system that had been built up for one thousand to two thousand years—was destroyed and never fully reconstructed.

In the middle of this devastation there was a great task that had to be done: the reconstructing and restoring of the means of life to people—the renewing of the agriculture that had been devastated and the rebuilding of the cities. This was undertaken largely with the help of a group of disciples of Abd al-Khaliq, some of whom became famous as great saints and teachers, and who are known in the East as the "masters of wisdom." For two hundred or three hundred years they continued to play a great role and finally succeeded in establishing a long period of peace in Central Asia, until the eighteenth century when Central Asia was invaded by Russia.

Gurdjieff also used the term fourth way with much this idea: that there is open to everyone the possibility of seeking their own spiritual development by their own efforts through devotion to a teacher, by intellectual search, by asceticism and self-denial, or by withdrawal from the world, but that there is also a fourth way, and it is only active— only fully active—when there is a task to be done.

His emphasis on this part of it connects it with that earlier notion that I have been talking about:: the notion of a task of some service that is required and needed in a certain place, as it was needed in the whole of Central Asia at the time of the Mongol invasion. We should recognize that there is a "way" that is essentially a "way of service"— not service in the external sense only, but service also in the sense of sustaining the morale and confidence of a people who were then completely shattered by the invasion, the destruction, and the terrible loss of life.

The destruction may not always be on such a great scale as in the time of Genghis Khan and the Mongol invasions. The same thing happened on a somewhat smaller scale two centuries later with Tamerlane (Amir Timur) when there was again a great devastation, and again there was reconstruction by the successors of the same masters. At that time this era of peace about which I have spoken was inaugurated. The whole thing lasted about five hundred years and was an extraordinary event that has not been sufficiently studied nor understood, though it has a lot to teach us about our present problems. This is not, of course, the only example of a group of wise and enlightened men who have been able to help a region through a time of great crisis. It has happened several times in recorded history.

Now, how does all that apply to our present time, if at all? People do recognize that we are passing through a difficult period—and even a period of crisis—and they do see that our way of life is threatened. But I think that on the whole we are like the people of Bokhara and Samarkhand who refused to believe that it could happen. They did not believe that it was possible that the whole of their way of life would disappear in the course of two or three years, or that there would be such wholesale loss of life. Today we think that we are going through a difficult period but that it will not lead to the degree of devastation and destruction that perhaps some are forecasting. Maybe not, but there are reasons for believing that the changes will be greater than people are willing to admit.

One change that I will speak about because I shall come back to it later is on the subject of food. It is generally recognized that we are entering a period of food shortage; combined with the rapid growth of population, this is going to be serious. But it is also quite widely assumed that we can, just by turning on the tap of technology, increase our food production to any desired degree. This is not true: our present expansion of agriculture has largely been a matter of chemistry and engineering, and it is to an extraordinary degree dependent upon petroleum products. The enormous expansion of fertilizer production and the increasing dependence of agriculture upon machinery has made agriculture almost entirely dependent upon abundant and cheap supplies of petroleum products. We are already beginning to notice the effect of the increased cost of petroleum products and its repercussions for agriculture, but we think of it only as a matter of cost and that it will be possible to find some way out of this.

But the truth is that if we were to attempt to do what was apparently called for yesterday by a high-ranking U.S. statesman—that is, to double the production of food in twenty years—we would use all the available supplies of oil. The calculation can readily be made that it is just not within technical possibility, because the resources are not there—either to make the fertilizer or to provide the transport and machinery that is needed. What is also notorious is the threatened loss of the fertility of the land through overcultivation. But people do not wish to look at this. It is interesting to see that this kind of statement— that we must double our food production—can be made by eminent people when any expert can tell them, and probably in private does tell them, that they are talking nonsense.

If we are in fact entering a period of an overall devastating food shortage that will result in death by starvation of hundreds of millions of people, then it does mean that the world is coming to a crisis comparable to that of thirteenth-century Central Asia—but on a world scale instead of just the main land area of the world that is Asia.

This refusal of people to accept any presentation of the situation that is disturbing to them is totally characteristic of man. It is not something new. At all times man has had this peculiar weakness of not wishing to face facts and of being determined to continue to live in a dream world. This is one of the things of special importance that we learned from Gurdjieff when he came to the West fifty years ago.

It was to me a devastating shock when I became associated with world affairs on a political scale to see that people were not facing the facts. I watched the first peace treaties being written after the 1914– 18 war, and wherever I had some real knowledge, as I did of the Near and Middle East, I saw that they were just writing formality for a new war. Yet they were talking of making a lasting peace in the world. So I became convinced that one of the great problems facing mankind is this refusal to face disagreeable facts and the readiness to listen to anyone who will give comforting assurances.

But I presume that most of you who have come here have come to much the same kind of conclusion. You do see for yourselves that we are in front of a situation that will inevitably lead to a very great cataclysm in human affairs and that we have to prepare ourselves to live through this or, in the least, prepare something that can be different for our children and for those who come after us. This is the task that every sane, serious, thinking person must face, and what are we all to do in front of it?

We have, at the present time, a society that is based on growth, on the worship of size. Everything bigger is taken to be better. Progress means increasing size; progress is synonymous with growth. We have to see, all of us, the absurdity of this. This is a totally fictitious progress that at all times has been harmful but at the present time is going to be fatal. How can we do anything to prepare for a state of affairs in which this is reversed, in which we turn away from bigness for its own sake—from growth for its own sake, from the gospel of "more"—to the gospel of "enough," of being satisfied with the least and with what is necessary? This requires a self-discipline for which people are not prepared. From childhood we are brought up to ask for more, to look upon it as a merit to get more if one can get it. If one is able to take, one takes. This is what we are taught. Not only by the bad example of all adults but even by teaching, by precept. How are we, who are so conditioned to live by grasping for more, to turn toward a way of life in which we are satisfied with less? It is clearly useless to talk about this, to tell people that we ought to give up this grasping for more. We can see without any doubt that human beings are not capable of this. This deeply bred atavistic behavior—maybe it is more; maybe it is in our very animal nature—that we take if we can take can be overcome only if we change ourselves.

And we have to face something else: that not only is the world in difficulties but these difficulties cannot be overcome from the outside by anything that we can do, or that anyone can do, as long as people themselves do not change. But the great majority of people will not change and do not wish to change. Can the few, therefore, who wish to change make any contribution? Are they not such a small minority that they might as well retire and look after themselves?

This is where we come back to this notion of a fourth way. The Fourth Way is not only a way of service, but it is also a way of "self-perfecting," of "self-transformation." It is necessary for people who wish to serve to be able to sacrifice. Anyone can sacrifice in a splendid way when everyone's eye is on them. But the small, daily sacrifice of doing without this or that, of allowing oneself to be imposed on, to allow others to get the better of us, to give up our pride, sometimes even to give up our self-respect—that sort of sacrifice doesn't come without a very great inward change. And one must know that *that* change is necessary and be prepared to commit oneself to it. Only people who are committed to that change can be said to be "people of the way." Whichever "way" it is, whether it is the ways that turn away from the world, that look for personal perfecting, or whether it is this Fourth Way, which is the way of service and of work in the world, it is only those people who are committed to changing themselves who can follow it. And especially if we wish to serve, we must know, as many of us have learned, perhaps, in the hard way, that we cannot do it so long as we remain as we are. We have to change.

For this reason, an essential element of the Fourth Way is the teaching of *how to change*—giving people the know-how, creating the conditions in which they can change themselves. If there is a task to be undertaken—a practical task in the world—it is first of all necessary that one should have the required skills. One has to be competent; good will is not enough. One cannot restore agriculture unless one has thorough knowledge of the foundation of agriculture, as Ubeydullah Hahah did in the fifteenth century when he restored the agriculture of Transoxania. Ubeydullah Hahah was one of the greatest of the masters. Although his youth was devoted entirely to his spiritual development and the overcoming of his own egoism, when he saw the need for the restoration of agriculture in the face of the destruction of the irrigation system, he set himself to study how irrigation systems could be improvised. As a result, when there was a great food shortage, he saved the lives of hundreds of thousands, if not millions.

This is the first thing one must be in order to be able to serve: one must be a practical person. In addition, one must be able to overcome the wish to be *something* in oneself, because this wish puts us in conflict with others. We have, somehow or other, to get out of ourselves the desire to shine, the desire to be something, to be appreciated, to have the satisfaction of a visible achievement. We have to be able to tolerate other people and tolerate them completely—not just externally but by accepting them as they are, without attempting to impose ourselves on them.

All of this is not easy. But at all times this has been recognized by those of the Fourth Way, and from this comes the concept of schools of the Fourth Way, schools where this can be taught, where people can be shown how to overcome their own defects, how to develop their powers, how to become more effective in their action of service. This was the striking thing about the Fourth Way schools. I have taken it to illustrate what I am talking about because much information is available as to how these masters of wisdom of Central Asia taught and the methods they used—how they combined the teaching of skills with the development of the powers in people and how they helped people to find a way to overcome their own weaknesses and egoism. Fortunately, this knowledge was preserved even after Central Asia had been invaded by the Russians, and the masters continued teaching right up until the beginning of this century.

We owe a great deal to Gurdjieff, who, at the end of the last century and the beginning of this century, was able to go to Central Asia and find the remains of these teachings—and to come into contact with not only the teachings but also the people. I first came across this concept of the Fourth Way in 1923 when I spent some time with Gurdjieff in France. He spoke to me then—that's fifty-one years ago— about the need to prepare for the situation that was going to arise in the world. He said that another world war was inevitable; that there would be a great social collapse; that it would be necessary to prepare, as others had done in the past; and that *this* was the mission he felt he had to undertake. But his life was such that he was never able to accomplish what he set out to do. Now it remains for others to follow it, and this is why I'm here, speaking to you today.

Now, what is the task that is in front of us, and what is the task that I want to speak to you about?

We have at this time a culture that is based upon large institutions. It is primarily an economic culture and, as I have said before, a culture of growth and expansion that requires and encourages large institutions. But when growth ceases to be easy because resources are restricted, then large institutions get into trouble, as we see them getting into trouble today.

We are living in a culture, also, of large cities. There are great cities in the world with millions of inhabitants; this is something new in the history of the world. Even great cities of the past, such as Rome and Babylon, were quite small compared with modern cities. These cities are made possible solely by transportation. It was only when transportation became easy through the discovery of steam, and thereafter of the internal combustion engine, that it was possible to convey food and commodities in and out of large cities in the way we do today. These things all require large-scale organizations, and all over the world these organizations are getting into trouble and will get into worse trouble.

Therefore, the task before us is to see *what kind of society can arise in the midst of this.* When I first spoke about this last year, I compared our present society to a dinosaur culture where the giant institutions are like the great reptiles of the Cretaceous period. They were able to flourish in a favorable climate, just as the climate of growth today is favorable to great institutions. They were, however, replaced by the mammals, who had an incomparably greater power of adaptation to change and could live in unfavorable conditions.

As someone said to me today, it wasn't the antelopes that killed off the dinosaurs. And it will not be a new society that would enter into conflict with the old society or attempt to replace it that will kill off the old society. The old society will die by itself as growth ceases to be possible. What will replace it will be a society based upon a greater degree of decentralization, which will restore agriculture to its rightful place in the life of man. Much smaller communities with sufficiently diversified activity to give a full and rich life to its members will arise, and they will not be dependent upon large-scale technology, or at least not as dependent as at present. Maybe one could go even further and say that there would be no reason for the present scale to diminish if people were wise. All that one can say with confidence is that the scale can't double. There is not the means for it. That is certain. So it's not a matter of conflict between an old society and a new, but rather the emerging of a society that will be viable, that will be able to live under the conditions that will come into the world in the next hundred or two hundred years. . . .

Many people all over the world at the present moment are thinking of these things that I am talking to you about. Tens of thousands of small communities are being set up in many different countries with this same idea of returning to the land, turning away from large-scale mechanization and industry. When one looks at those, then one sees another side—that is, almost invariable failure. These communities last a short time and then fail; very few prove to be viable.

Why is this? The ideas are good. The people go with a sense of devotion. But there are two mistakes that are generally made. The first mistake is to think that one can do without technology altogether, that one can just turn one's back on the modern world and live naturally on the model of Gandhi or Tolstoy. This is not possible. One cannot dispense with what is known in a world that is so overpopulated as ours. Therefore there can't be this separation between the new and the old that some people are looking for.

The other, much more serious, mistake is that the psychological difficulties of living in a community are always underestimated. The enthusiasm with which a community is started doesn't survive. There is either too much success or too much failure. Too often these communities are dependent upon some individual who has a capacity for leadership, for inspiration, but who also has a desire to dominate or who can't overcome the tendency to dominate—and then, again, impossible situations arise.

Therefore, the attempts that are being made all over the world to solve this and to create some kind of New Age society are—one must face it—proving very unsuccessful, mainly through lack of know-how—not only technical know-how but psychological and spiritual know-how. That is where we come back again to this notion of the Fourth Way.

The Fourth Way combines the outer and the inner: the outward service with the inner transformation. It offers people the possibility of changing themselves, because people who are not, at least, in the process of self-perfecting, of self-transformation, cannot effectively work together unless they are under some threat or unless they are promised some reward. However much they may wish to do so, they cannot as a pure act of service work together as is necessary. That knowledge has to be taken into account. That is why there are schools where people are shown how they can, as it is put, "work on themselves." But these schools of the Fourth Way are essentially geared to performing a task. They have no other justification. They don't exist just to teach or to transmit knowledge or to give people individual opportunities of self-perfecting. They exist because there is a work to be done.

I think it doesn't require any kind of inspiration from above to see that there is, in front of us all, a work to be done, which is to discover the kind of society that is going to be needed in the future and to show how that society will work. In my vision of it, there is no doubt that this society will be a much more decentralized society consisting of units that are far less dependent upon large-scale technology and large institutions than our present society is. But it will not be a society that will turn its back on these. There will be a very long period when these will coexist. But these societies—the new societies—will not be concerned with only their own preservation or with only preparing for the future. I think that the restoration of food production to a natural basis is the more specific task that societies will have to undertake.

It is now possible, with the knowledge we have, to take care of the land and to produce food without the present dependence upon petroleum products. It is possible to produce a great deal more food by natural methods than is being done at present, but that means a more labor-intensive food production. Instead of the present situation, in which as few as 5 percent of the people produce by mechanization the food that is required for an industrial population, having the result that the other 95 percent get crowded into cities where they live miserably, it is possible for people to engage to a far greater extent in food production, to have a more satisfying life on that very account, and to have better-quality food—providing, of course, that we don't make the same mistake that is being made today, of making it all intolerably dull. And it is! Agriculture is becoming intolerably dull, and this is really the chief reason for the flight from the land. To make the production of food interesting, it must be undertaken by communities that have other interests. This is why we are proposing to make an experiment in this direction.

For many years in the institute* of which I am director—since the end of the last war, in fact—we have been investigating the different religious and spiritual movements of the world, looking at the know-how and the methods that are followed, and we have been drawn more and more to the wisdom of Central Asia and the methods that we have learned chiefly through Gurdjieff and through my own contacts with schools in Central Asia. Out of this experience that we have gained here in London at Kingston, we set up four years ago a school in Gloucestershire at Sherborne. Its purpose is to prepare people who are willing and who wish to learn how to work on themselves. We should call them "candidates for the new society."

This has given extremely promising results—with ups and downs but results better than I had personally hoped for—so that now there are several hundred people who have had this experience, and this will continue. But it is only the first stage of the experiment because it is concerned only with teaching people *how* it is possible to work for their own self-perfecting and *how* it is possible to develop a "group consciousness" or sense of unity of a "group working for a common aim." *That* I can say *is* possible; and we have shown it to be possible from this experience.

We have further set ourselves to see if we can come to a "working society," based upon the principles that I have been talking about. And

* The Institute for the Comparative Study of History, Philosophy and the Sciences, Ltd.

I am able now to speak to you about it because I just came back, a couple of days ago, from America, where we have entered into an agreement to buy a large tract of land in West Virginia,* about sixty miles from Washington, D.C. The land has many facilities for development, and there is the possibility of acquiring further land. Thanks to there being many buildings on this property—so we don't have to spend time in building—we hope to be able to begin next October with a school** like the one we have in Gloucestershire.

We hope also to start work on creating a society that will be largely self-supporting, aiming to arrive at a society of eight hundred to one thousand people. There is always a certain optimum or desirable size— for a Fourth Way school there shouldn't exceed about one hundred people—because there has to be a great deal of personal contact. Similarly, for a society, in order to get the necessary diversity so that everyone can have things that are of interest to them, a larger number is required. And, of course, families have to be accommodated and be able to live and work together.

Here I come up against the question, Where is the kind of knowledge for making such societies viable to come from? This is something about which I can't say I have had very much experience. I have been engaged in the psychological and spiritual side of the work, so I was extremely thankful when I became aware of the valuable work that was being done by an old friend of mine, Dr. Schumacher—some of you may have read his book *Small is Beautiful*—and of his work with intermediate technology, which is now producing quite remarkable results for the very purpose of enabling relatively small communities to make themselves self-supporting.

I will give you just one example, which he told me about today, of an experiment that is being made in America. You may have heard of Dr. Todd in Massachusetts, who is producing food from fish with the help of a source of foodstuff for the fish themselves. This was of special interest to me because at this new place at Claymont Court in West Virginia we have large springs and quite a considerable flow of water, and I hoped we should be able to produce something in the way of a fishery, but I didn't see how we were to feed them. Dr. Todd's experiment consists in establishing a dome over a pond to concentrate

*Claymont Court, an historic mansion, originally built by Bushrod Corbin Washington, a great nephew of George Washington.
**The Claymont School for Continuous Education was inaugurated in October 1975 under the direction of Dr. Pierre Elliot. J.G. Bennett died in December of 1974.

sunshine and maintain a high temperature for the production of plankton or algae at about thirty or forty times their normal rate. And from this he is successfully providing all the food that is needed for his fish farm. This form of technology is the kind that I think is of very great interest to us . . . and is a great part of the secret of changing our agricultural production so that it will not be dependent upon large-scale mechanized technology, yet it will be no less efficient than it is today. We hope that we shall be able to do research and development in these directions. But even where we have this know-how that people are very willing to share with one another, we still come back to the problem of the human being. This must, above all, be faced.

The world will not change unless people change. And people will not change until they see the necessity for it. We have examples: those of us who are old enough to remember the last war and those who remember the first war can remember what happened to people under *those* really dreadful, totally absurd conditions. With the loss of the usual forms of discipline, people developed a quite new relationship: everyone became as brothers in the front line, and there came to be a fellowship and a readiness to share with one another.

When the war ended, after the bombardment of London, I prayed, "Can we keep this feeling of good will toward one another, at least enough to avoid relapsing into the cut-throat life that we had before?" But within twelve months everything had gone: we were, everyone of us, grasping again. Strong and weak, rich and poor, all alike—everyone had gone back to the complete selfishness that characterizes human life.

One might from that experience become hopeless and say, "What can be done? This race doesn't deserve to live." But it does. It has very good things in it, this human race, and it is destined for a very high purpose in this world. This earth has got a great destiny in front of it, and man is the core of that destiny. Man is in a very early stage of his evolution. He has only really humanized to a very small degree—and relatively few truly *human* beings exist in the world. But this great destiny will come. For this, we have to survive. For this, we have to make a step forward. That is the only true progress. The only true progress is the progress toward becoming human beings, not beasts. For this, confidence has to be given. And that, I think, is the most important task of all.

It is not enough to show that a community can be formed that will be viable, that people will tolerate one another and live together because they have an interesting and diversified life, and that they are not dominated by great cities and the rest of it. Beyond that, it is necessary to give people—to give all of us—the confidence that there is a "higher power," a spiritual power working in the world with which we can cooperate, that is helping us, that is concerned with the future of mankind, that by no means has given up hope for man, and that is, in fact, now working. I think that this is the key to it all: that that confidence should grow in us, because confidence communicates; confidence spreads. If one ceases to believe that there is a spiritual power, then hope goes. When this belief returns and people can show by their lives that they do believe in it, then hope returns not only to them but to many others. This is the task that I see.

✧

Answers to Questions

MORE IMPORTANT THAN THE BIRTH RATE, more important than the effect of hygiene on prolonging life, is our human egoism and selfishness. We could do much better. I find it difficult to answer your question about this because when one says "duty" and "ought," I feel that one must always ask oneself, "What can one do?" The things that I have been speaking to you about are all things that I and my friends can and will do. But if you say to me, "Is it a duty to reduce the birthrate in the world?" I must say to you, "Whose duty?" Are you going to go and preach to people that they must reduce the birthrate without telling them something that will make it possible for them to do it? I think that we are going to go through a period that is going to be very difficult, because the birthrate will not substantially reduce and we shall get to a population that will involve a great deal of death from starvation. I think that is inevitable, and we must face it that hundreds of millions of people will die of starvation in the next twenty-five years. This will then itself create a pressure to change the situation.

I do not see any other way by which this reduction of population can come about, because people will not respond to being told what they *ought* to do. After all, you and I don't—let's be truthful about it. We have been told how we ought to live. If we look at ourselves, are we using the resources that are available to us in a way that is compatible with the needs of the whole world? Are we exercising the degree of self-restraint that would be necessary to be exercised by everyone for this world to be viable? We are not. Very few people are. There are very few people who are capable of doing what they ought to do;

therefore, how can we venture to tell people what their duty is if we are not able to do our own? This, I think, has to be faced.

Your first question about whether this is an "unprecedented situation"—I think it is. It is connected with time, and I think that that is another subject. We have reached a stage of accelerated change when, for the first time in history, there has been a complete change in the social environment within one person's lifetime. The world as it was before 1914, which I can remember, is unrecognizably different from the world of today. In that sense there is an unprecedented situation. The other thing that is unprecedented is the totality of the situation. It is not regional anymore. There has never before been something like that. And therefore one has to ask oneself how it has come about that we are living in a time that is like that. That is in itself a most interesting and important subject: What characterizes our "time," this present time, and that period of a century or two that makes it different from any other part of recorded history?

But it is different. And this I am certain of, and I am certain that I can see why it is so, why it is that we are now facing something unprecedented. And we can't look back to the past and say that trouble in one area has been compensated by the relative stability in another. The world is no longer like that.

. . . What is remarkable about China is how much more natural their agriculture is and how effective. With such a huge population—in a country no bigger than the United States and four times the population—they are able to manage a far more natural food production than the rest of the world. It is an achievement. And there is, of course, a great deal of decentralization. The village communities do have a life that doesn't lead to this flight from the land that we have. But we are dealing with our problem. If you are suggesting that China will be exempt from the troubles that the rest of the world is going through, I don't know. Some people do believe that, but I don't know. What I do know is that we have a task in front of us, and that task is the one that concerns me.

The small societies exist in many parts of the world. The villages are there; it's a matter of preserving them. We have this assumption that growth and expansion are things that are to be desired and that what we call the developing countries are somehow backward because they are not growing as fast and wasting as many resources as the rest of the world. I think that what they need above all is the know-how. Already a great deal of this work of intermediate technology is beginning to benefit other countries, particularly the developing countries.

We can do what we can do. I can see in front of myself this possibility of starting one experiment now. If that works it can serve as a model, and the lessons that we shall learn from it will be available to everyone if we can get people trained—and I say this with great emphasis, because untrained and unprepared people can't do this. To rush into making a community with all sorts of technical ideas of small-scale technology without the basic training is asking for failure. Therefore, the rate at which this can spread depends upon how many people are willing to be trained and how quickly they can be, because it requires also a great deal of experience to help people and it has taken many years to get people together with the necessary experience. One has to look at it in this way: that every great change in the world has begun in a small way. Nothing really good has ever begun large. The great mistake is to think that because something is good it will be better to do it quickly and on a big scale. People say, "But why, if things are so urgent, if there is such a desperate situation coming up, why can't we mobilize greater resources?" The answer is that size is itself an obstacle. You cannot go faster than the natural growth.

. . . Supposing that there were some possibility of changing the gestation period so that a woman could produce a child in a fortnight instead of ten months. Do we really think that that would be a great step forward? There would be so many more chances, so much greater risk, of producing monsters if that were to happen that nobody would dream of doing it. And yet we try to do other things too fast, and we do produce monsters. There is a natural rate of growth and one must be patient. One must not try to go faster. We have to learn to look at the world on a greater time scale. It is perhaps not even in our own lifetimes that we must look.

We must look at the world for the next five hundred years and see whether there will be a better humanity in the world, on this earth, than there is today. If that can be, if we can make even a small contribution toward that, our lives will have been justified. If we try to do too much too quickly, we shall produce monsters. This may be very hard to accept but only if you don't see the laws of true transformation. There is talk, of course, of sudden, immediate transformation. This is also not right. Everything requires its own time.

. . . Man didn't come into this world for nothing. Man is an extraordinary achievement that has required long and difficult preparation. This achievement is not complete. It would be quite a considerable cosmic disaster if this experiment with man on this earth were to fail, and for this reason much is being done to prevent this experiment from failing—not because man deserves to survive, but because he is really needed.

However much we may criticize man, we have to realize how difficult it is to be a man. People don't really grasp this. It is exceedingly hard to be, in the true sense, a man, a human being. We are given powers, creative powers, that are necessary, but they are terribly dangerous. Man has also got a freedom that is necessary but terribly dangerous, and it is not right to have a hostile or negative attitude toward the human race. The higher powers do not have it, and we shouldn't have it either. One should, on the contrary, have great compassion, great love for mankind, this struggling creature that is trying to fulfill an almost impossible destiny. We should not feel hostile. In spite of our arrogance, in spite of our selfishness, there is this struggle that is going on in the world. Many, many people try to make something better of their lives. Unless we feel great compassion for mankind, we can't do our work in this world.

Any kind of hostility, any kind of rejection of our fellowmen, is against the high purpose, and we shouldn't serve mankind with a feeling of superiority because we are better, because we happen to see something, or because we have a higher ideal. It is not like that. We are not better. I am no better than any other man because I am a man—I am not something else. And we are all in the same boat. That feeling that we are all in the same boat must be strong with us. Only in that way can we really have compassion.

So, thank you very much.

✧

SHERBORNE HOUSE   *Photograph by Joseph Stoner*

Sherborne House was the location of the International Academy for Continuous Education from 1971 to 1976. This Victorian mansion, nestled among the lush green hills of the Cotswold district of England was annually the home of more than one hundred adults and children from around the world. This community of diverse people formed a Fourth Way school, which was an "experiment" in transmitting techniques for spiritual transformation and awakening in human beings their potential for service to life.

PROGRESS IN
SELF-PERFECTING is not
automatic, it requires the use of
the right methods and the
determination to persevere
against all discouragements.

—From *A Call for a New Society*
J.G. Bennett's manifesto for a psychokinetic
society, November 1974.

Inaugural Address
Second Basic Course, 1972–73

J.G. Bennett's introductory talk to students at the International
Academy for Continuous Education.*

WHY HAVE WE COME TOGETHER, and what do we hope to do in
the year we shall spend together? There are two questions to be
answered here. One is what kind of person we want to be and
whether we can find the means here of making a step toward becoming that kind of human being. The other is what kind of a world we
want to live in—for ourselves, our children, and our children's children.
Can we find here the way to make some contribution to creating that
world? If there were not both of these questions to be answered, I
think I would not be here; I would not feel that it was my duty to
devote my declining years solely to help you become a particular kind
of person, though this is an important and necessary task. It is because
I have the conviction that it is even more important that we should
turn our attention to the kind of world that we want to see, to live in,
that I am here and am ready to give the whole of my powers, as far as
they go, to helping you find an answer to your own questions. I hope
also that we shall go some way toward an answer to the question we
all must share: that is, what kind of a world are we going toward, and
can we do something to make it more like the kind of world we want
to live in?

The kind of person that each one of us wants to be is really his
own business. The choice is left to us. This is what it means to be a
man. He has the power to choose what kind of a being he is going to
become, what kind of a life he is going to live. That kind of being is
rather rare in the universe. Most are allotted tasks in the cosmic order,
and they are formed in such a way that they have to play their part in

*Originally published in 1973 by the Institute for the Comparative Study of
History, Philosophy and the Sciences, Ltd., Gloucestershire, England. The
Institute is no longer active.

it. Failure for them can be only failure of the environment to provide them with the conditions. An acorn will become an oak; it will become nothing else but an oak, providing the environment allows it. A lamb will become a sheep; a worm will become a worm. These are all serious cosmic roles that have to be filled. Without trees, without sheep, without worms, this earth would not be able to fulfill its destiny, and the same is true of all the other kinds of beings. There are also, I am sure, beings of a higher order than man, who are also allotted tasks, and they, too, are formed in such a way that they will fulfill these tasks according to a higher will, with comparatively little choice as to what they themselves will be. This may be so because their task is of such importance that it has to be filled just as it is allotted to them.

But we men are different. We men are confronted with the power, each one of us, to decide what kind of a human being we are going to be. All of us have an ideal and hopes for what we will become, but we know precious little about how to achieve it and how to equip ourselves to fill the part that we would like to fill. Until a person has awakened perceptions that enable him to see it, even the path he has to follow is hidden from him. A peculiar thing characterizes us: every human being has a cosmic role to fill, and we don't know what it is. We do not know how to prepare ourselves for it, and yet inwardly everyone of us—and especially everyone of us gathered together here—has a deep conviction that there is something we have to do with our lives. Each one of you knows that there is something that you have to find out about yourself and what you ought to be and that there is something that you need to know about how you become what you ought to be.

It is very strange that man should be put in this predicament, convinced that there's something important that he ought to know about himself and about the way he should be living his life, yet a veil is drawn that hides from him a great part of what he most needs to know. All the guidance he has is the past history of mankind, the ways in which people have lived before us, the way they thought it right to live, and the way that they laid down that people ought to live. In most stages of the earth's history, this will pass fairly well, but moments come when it no longer works. Circumstances are changing profoundly, and the old precedents, the old traditions, the old rules and commandments no longer apply in the way that they have been understood before. These transitions have occurred over and over again in human history. They are moments of very great interest and significance, when the search for the ability to fill one's own role becomes more significant than at any other time.

We are in such a period of history when our inadequacy becomes painfully obvious. We know this but do not understand why there is this deep feeling that everyone shares, whether they are willing to admit it or not. It is there, whether we hide it from ourselves and from others successfully or not. Deep down we know that something is missing. This makes us afraid—afraid in front of other people, in front of the world. Again we try to hide this fear from ourselves. This is the real crux of our situation: we know that something is not quite right or something is missing, but we do not know what it is. We put the best face on it. We do not know how to find this out.

This does not mean that we do not also know that there is much we can do to change our situation. We know very well that there is much to learn, that we need to get more control over ourselves, more understanding, and more sympathy with other people. We know that we are the slaves of many undesirable habits, and we would like to correct these things, but there is something deeper. It is the awareness that we are called to something that we are not able to respond to.

In this there is no difference between people except in the degree to which they can turn their backs on this situation and forget it and live without facing the question. For such people it is the outer world that is the trouble. If things go wrong, it is because of other people, because of circumstances, because of misfortunes, or at the most because of mistakes that they make because they have not seen what to do. But those mistakes that they acknowledge are still well outside the real deep awareness that there is something in us that is missing. People who are able to live in this way, without concerning themselves with the deep question, can in one sense be called fortunate, because they are free from the torture that people have to suffer for whom this question begins to burn. They can be very effective, they can be successful in life, and they can convince themselves that their success satisfies them. They can do this in other people's eyes. They can see that they are admired and imitated, and with that they feel that they have evidence that all is well with them.

But, as they grow older, the time comes, perhaps moments come, when this question reappears for them, and that is no joke, because they see that the time for finding an answer to it has passed. But there are many, many people for whom the question does not arise at all and who go contentedly to the grave, thinking that they have made a success of their lives. And in one sense they have. Perhaps that is what they were intended to do, and perhaps that is the role they were intended to fill. It may be even that the inability to be aware of the deep questions was given to them to enable them to fill the role.

Let us take it that we who are here do ask this question and that we know that we will not be satisfied if we cannot find something more to do with our lives than making a successful impact on our society. One thing we shall try to do in this course here is to reach the point where we can face this question together and begin to see for ourselves something that cannot be conveyed by words or explanations but only by an inner vision of the emptiness in us and how we are to pass through it and find the "reality" that is beyond it. If I can help you toward this, this will be the most important achievement possible. A fair proportion of the people who came last year were able to do this, and this is more comforting perhaps than when we started a year ago, when I was obliged to say to everyone that I could not tell whether what we were setting out to do could be accomplished in ten short months, because I had never seen it attempted before.

I believe that it can be done and that those of you who have the necessary qualities and aptitudes can hope to achieve it. Others may not come to it this year, but if you are well grounded you will come to it later.

I have spoken of the deeper significance of our work. This will not arise at first. There is much to be prepared, and the preparation itself is progress. The work is traditionally divided into three phases, which we call the exoteric, mesoteric, and esoteric phases. By exoteric, we mean coming to terms with the outward problems of our own nature, coming to know ourselves as human machines—to know how our bodies and our feelings and our minds work—and learning to some extent how to control ourselves. In this phase we also set ourselves to understand the principles that are true for us all. Those can be conveyed by talk or by illustration, or by experiments of different sorts, just because they represent part of the world in which we all share and that is within reach of our knowing power. If this goes fairly well according to pattern, it will take two or three months.

After that, we come to the mesoteric phase, when we seek to penetrate more deeply into our own nature and begin to understand for ourselves how it is that we are not in touch with our own reality. This is a matter of *seeing*. We in our modern English usage take the word *theoretical* in an abstract sense, but in old Greek *theoria* means a way of seeing that was objective, as distinct from the ordinary subjective *opsis*. The divine seeing in us has to be awakened. Then we begin to be able to face the real problem and see that it is this very thing that is the cause of the fear of people and their lack of confidence in themselves, which makes them timid or bombastic, active or passive, dominates them from behind the scenes without their being aware of it, and produces in them all the foolish manifestations of man. We see that facing this is the gateway to reality, and so far from fearing it, it is through that gate we have to go.

Those who can—and I have no means whatever of predicting whether any one or ten or even most of you can do that—will come to the point where they will enter the world of reality. This is called the esoteric phase. Whether this takes ten months or ten years does not matter. If it takes a whole lifetime but is achieved in the end, that is a successful life in the objective sense. It is successful not in the external, visible sense, but in the cosmic sense: a life that has awakened to reality and learned how to live in that world. Such a one becomes a cosmic being of a different order from ordinary men and women. It would be absurd to suggest that we could do more than put our feet on this path during this year. But if we achieve that, it is then for each one of us to follow it if we can.

The other question I put to you is, "What kind of a world is it that we want to see? What kind of a world would we wish to live in, to see coming for our children and our children's children?" From this standpoint, it is not my life or your life that matters—it is the life of mankind, of our children on earth who will come after us. There are probably not many of you here—I doubt if there is a single one—who thinks that this world in which we are living at this moment is an acceptable world that we would wish to have if we had the power to choose. There is something very wrong with it.

One reason why the world is wrong is, of course, that the people who live in it now are not facing reality. They are facing reality neither in themselves nor in the world of events. Matters that require to be looked at in the time scale of centuries are pushed out of sight. Matters that must be looked at in the scale of decades are disregarded. People live for the moment. We stumble from crisis to crisis, and the larger the organization, the worse is this tendency to avoid facing the big issues and deal only with the small things. I learned this lesson fifty-two years ago when I happened to be an interpreter to a peace conference and had to stand behind all the big men of the age—President Wilson and Lloyd George and Clemenceau and Sforza and all the people who were determining, as they thought, the future of the world—and saw with my own eyes how these great men of the world were moved by petty jealousies, unworthy personal considerations, and even by sex and money.

At the very time I was seeing all this in front of me, I was also going, whenever I could, to the lectures Ouspensky was giving, in which he was saying, "Man cannot do. Man has no control over his destiny. Man doesn't understand himself what is happening to him. He is a machine. He is asleep!" And it was strange for me to see, during the daytime, how everything I had heard from Ouspensky the previous evening was being verified before my very eyes. Soon we began to verify it all for ourselves. We saw how far we were from being the kind of person that we imagined or that other people assumed that we were. We saw how unwilling anyone is to face the reality of it all.

But there are more specific things we can see in this world. One trouble is that people are the slaves of their feelings and are not able to act from their reason. They are not able to make compromises, accept difficult and embarrassing situations according to sane reason, simply because their feelings are too weak. Their minds become the slaves of these weak feelings of theirs, and the result is that they go from one trouble into another, unable to "grasp nettles" and be stung a little in order not to incur a great deal of harm.

We live in this world by the very nature of existence—not just the economy of this earth, but by the nature of all existence in space and time—in a state of corporeal limitation. We are limited by the fact of living in a body, where everything is measured in quantities. There is one inescapable fact, and that is that the things that *can* happen are very much fewer than the things that *might* happen; therefore, all that *could be* never *can be*. This translates itself into the simple proposition that *there can never be enough to go around*. Because we men have a great power of adaptation, if we choose to use it, there could be enough to go around if only we were prepared to discipline ourselves very severely and not grasp at everything we could take. We all know only too well that the world is not going that way, not by any means. And wherever there is power, there is grasping. Nobody is really willing to give. They are unwilling to give way, owing to their emotional weakness, to fear—because they fear to lose something. They have become attached to quantity and do not see that quantity has no significance and that the reality is all qualitative. Value is not in "how much?" but in "how real?"

You have all come here thoroughly conditioned by this grasping world. You have, unconsciously to a great extent, been conditioned to disregard the needs of others and to think only of yourselves. This is visible in the way you behave here. If you are not willing to struggle with this and to get free from it, what kind of example can you set to the world, and how can we have anything that would appear to show what the world could be?

In this place and time we have a world in miniature. When this course was being organized, I had to study the letters and reports of a large number of people who asked to come here. In accepting you, I tried to arrange it so that we had people as varied as possible, with varied ages and varied types, varied positions in the world. And on the whole it has worked out like that. We wanted to have children, and we have children, even more perhaps in proportion than the world has of children.

In this little world, then, that we have here, we have to ask ourselves if we are going to try to live according to a pattern in which it is possible for man to live satisfactorily—a pattern that embraces all people, not just you and me. That will be possible only if we deny ourselves. We are going to make the experiment of putting ourselves on exactly the same plan as others and never looking for more for ourselves than for someone else. The world must little by little be brought to understand that any other way of life will produce only conflict and eventually disaster.

What can we do? If we can satisfy ourselves that it is possible to live this way and we can taste for ourselves the satisfaction of living in that way, then we shall be entitled to speak to people and say that the world's present way of living is not the way of the future. My own experience of life has been that when I have given way and allowed myself to be imposed upon, it has always been good for me. Whenever I have refused to give way and tried to get things as I wanted them, it has always been bad for me. This experience has grown over a long life.

There are situations we shall study very soon, which I mention now because they concern the basis of our work. One of these is that one cannot be a satisfactory human being so long as one is dominated by likes and dislikes, by attraction and aversion. Such reactions are foreign to the true nature of man, who is not a polarized being, pulled in different directions by external forces. Yes/no, like/dislike, active/passive—these, called in the Bhagavad Gita the pairs of opposites, are so central to the possibility of becoming a normal human being that I speak about them in this introductory talk. If you are not prepared to do everything you can to struggle with your slavery to likes and dislikes, then it is of little use for you to be here.

In the ordinary way of life, we do the things that interest us and reject the things that do not interest us. For example, if you go to college, you will probably go to the lectures that interest you. If a course is dull or if something does not interest you, you keep away from it. Here, we ask you to do quite the opposite: to do particularly the things that you do not like and that do not interest you and, if you have to put everything aside, to put aside the things that do interest you and that you do want to do. If there are people here to whom you feel attracted and other people in whom you do not feel so interested or to whom you are not attracted, then we would ask you to turn your attention to these latter. If there are jobs to be done that you would prefer to avoid and jobs that you would like to do and that fascinate you in some way, then give special attention to the jobs you dislike and try to do them very well.

I shall say this to you yet again, and I am speaking from long experience that has shown me that nothing is more profitable in the stages of this work that lead one to the threshold of reality than working against likes and dislikes. If you are not prepared to do this and do not remember it constantly, you will be wasting your time here. There will be, of necessity, activities that do not interest you. Everyone will be tempted to say, "Well, that particular subject or that particular lecture does not interest me—now is the moment for me to go off and do some shopping or go off and mend my clothes" or something of this sort, or just simply, "I will have a rest because I am tired." Can you bring yourself to say, "No, this one that does not interest me is the one I will go to, and the one that interests me is the one that I will sacrifice"? If you do that, you will make real progress in what matters—that is, in your own being, in your own real self.

You must remember that you are not coming here to be "interested." You are not coming here to learn subjects that will be useful to you. You are coming here because you wish to be a real human being. And a real human being is one who is free—and one who is not free is not human. It is a special privilege and characteristic bestowed upon man that he has the right to be free, but he has to earn it. And he is not free if he is the slave of his likes and dislikes.

Of course, I do not mean by this that there is nothing useful to you all to be learned here. We hope very much that you will go away with many unexpected skills that you did not possess previously. You will be taught many things connected with the body, with the feelings, and with the mind. You will come to see the way they work and much deeper things that are not in the ordinary sense knowledge at all but a direct inner vision of *what is*.

Various things are arranged so that there will be opportunities. For example, let us suppose that something is made available in a quantity that is enough for everyone if each takes only his or her own share; then, if some people take more than their share and others have to go without, we shall have a picture of how the world is. Let us say some food is put out to be taken that everyone wants to eat and enjoy—and it is right that they should—but if those who come first take more than their fair share and those who come last do not get any at all, then you are repeating the characteristic behavior of the whole world at the present time. Everyone who can take, takes; those who cannot take, who have not the power to take, are left empty. That is the way of the world.

We must remind ourselves that the world we wish for is a just world. If we wish for a just world, then all our own actions must be just. Slaves cannot be just, only free people can be just. We shall have special opportunities of looking at the world situation, and we shall spend the last five or six weeks before we go preparing ourselves for the work we will do when we leave here: to make use of what we will have come to understand and what we will be able to do.

Let us just take one of the aphorisms that Gurdjieff put up in the Study House in his institute and that is also true here, namely, that "here we can only create conditions; we cannot do your work for you." And another thing that was written in the Study House was "You have come here to struggle only with yourself. Be thankful to anyone who gives you the opportunity to do so." I look around and see a lot of nice faces. I think it would be very much easier if there were a few real monsters here. We have all of us got a monster hidden somewhere, so maybe we can manage without any imported monsters.

What I have just said—that nobody can do your work for you—you have to take to heart. This is not an easy way. It is not easy to be responsible for oneself. It would not be so difficult if I were simply to make hard conditions that you would have to bear and feel very proud that you were able to bear our conditions, or if I were to behave like a monster and you were able to say, "Well, I can bear with him because he cannot be too monstrous for me." I have seen enough of that kind of thing myself to know that it doesn't really get us where we need to get to. The work has to come from within. It has to come from our own need, our own decision. Try to remember this; it is not easy. We shall have to work hard.

And we do have a wide range of activities from all kinds of practical work. This has been arranged, and we have every opportunity of doing practical things. Some of the people in last year's course said they felt sorry for you because you would not arrive in a stone-cold house with the kitchen ceiling collapsed and only one broken-down stove to cook for a hundred people. They feared that you would not know what the life here was like. I do not think that that is really necessary every time. We have got the stable block in front of us as a challenge, and we have a lot of work to do both inside and in the garden. Every one of these jobs provides an opportunity for working in a positive way: acquiring skills, improving attention, learning to work with other people, learning to work on all your functions—all the things that are useful.

In addition to this, we will do a good deal of work on the "movements." These are beautifully designed for developing not only the bodily powers of man but his complete balance of mind, body, feelings, and will. As much as possible, the theoretical background will be covered in the psychological meetings you will have with Dick Holland. Every week when we have our morning meetings, I will be showing you different exercises to work at and providing you with a theme for working on understanding together. We have a meeting tomorrow morning, when I will put before you the first theme for the first week, and on Friday evening we will begin to talk about what you have found in studying this.

I shall also be presenting various special subjects for study. I intend to repeat what we did last year in teaching you a language. I debated whether to teach Turkish or Sanskrit. There would have been interest in being able to recite the Gita in its own language or to learn some of the magnificent Vedic hymns. But there is more value in Turkish from the point of view of communication, because it is totally different from our European languages. Also, I am glad to say that I have been able to arrange with Henri Bortoft, who is a man of exceptional genius, to give two courses in Hermeneutics: the first will start fairly soon. And most of you have asked to have the opportunity of working with the Alexander people [the Alexander Technique for body alignment] with whom we are arranging to come here. So we shall have a very varied program. I shall be bringing in as well other experts for some specialized work.

So there won't be a lack of interesting things to do, but there will be, I hope—and I think we shall achieve it also—some uninteresting things to do. We'll give you the opportunity of doing things because you dislike them, not just because you like to. If we cannot come to the point where all people are the same and we have no more diffi-culty in making friends with or talking to Mr. X than to Mr. Y; where we have no barriers between us and different kinds of people; and where we have no barriers between us and different kinds of activity, where it is all the same thing to be a dustman or a prince—unless we attain that, we are not free.

Biographical Note

The Struggle to "Make Something" for Oneself

ALL BUT ONE OF THE TALKS in this book were given at the International Academy for Continuous Education in Sherborne, England, at the "experimental" Fourth Way school that J.G. Bennett established in 1971, less than four years before he died. Although many people had benefited from working and studying with him during the previous thirty years, it wasn't until he was at Sherborne that he set himself up as a teacher. The academy at Sherborne was the culmination of a spiritual search that had begun more than fifty years earlier and that had started to take shape from the time of his first meeting, in 1920, with the Russian teacher and philosopher George Ivanovitch Gurdjieff.

At Sherborne, in courses lasting only ten months, Bennett took on the task of trying to pass on—to one hundred students at a time—the fruits of his own lifetime's search. He felt it to be a task that he had been given and that there was a real need, especially among younger people, for the kind of practical knowledge and deep spiritual wisdom that he had earned during his eventful life.

It was a hazardous undertaking. Bennett didn't know whether it would be possible to convey anything of substance in so short a time, and he had neither candidates nor material resources. But in the summer of 1971, these quickly came together.

His teaching method was based on that developed in the early 1920s by Gurdjieff at the Institute for the Harmonious Development of Man at Fontainebleau in France. Students undertook practical work in the house and garden; they attended talks in which Bennett developed his own ideas; there were readings from Gurdjieff's writings and classes in his psychology, as well as intensive work on Gurdjieff's "Movements," an extraordinary repertoire of sacred and ritual dances. In addition, Bennett worked with Sufi techniques that he had learned directly from masters in the Middle East.

Bennett always referred to Sherborne and the "ideal human society" he envisioned in the last year of his life as "experiments." This word expresses his understanding of "hazard" as a factor that permeates all existence and gives it its "drama": thus he titled his great four-volume work *The Dramatic Universe.* Bennett understood hazard to give the danger of failure along with the possibility of progress, but he was not afraid of either one. In the course of his long search to make sense of the world and man's place within it, he tried many methods and consulted many sources of wisdom. Practical by nature, he was prepared to use these methods if he found by his own practice that they bore fruit or to abandon them if they did not.

The oldest of three children, J.G. Bennett was born June 8, 1897, of an American mother and an English father. His mother was from an old pre-Revolutionary New England family, and his father was a correspondent for Reuters, the international news agency. Though Bennett makes little reference in his autobiography, *Witness,* to his childhood, he acknowledges elsewhere that he owed his mother a great debt for instilling in him the virtues of hard work and tolerance.

Spending his early childhood in Italy, he learned to speak Italian before he spoke English. This lay the foundation for an extraordinary facility with languages, which later in his life enabled him to talk to many spiritual teachers (Gurdjieff among them) in their native tongues and to study Hindu, Buddhist, Islamic and Christian sacred texts in their original forms.

Formal education for Bennett stopped at school. He never took up the scholarship in mathematics that he won from Oxford University, for circumstances propelled him into life so fast that he never had time to go back. But he was an excellent sportsman and captained the school rugby football team. He went on to play for the army against such redoubtable opponents as the New Zealand national team. He broke his arm once and his collar bone twice in that robust sport, and he maintained that these experiences gave him, at an early age, a valuable freedom and indifference toward his own body.

In the First World War, at the age of twenty-one, Bennett became a captain in the Royal Engineers, with responsibility for signals and telegraphy. Reading his letters of the time, one is struck by a surprising indifference to the dangers he faced. One letter, to his fiancée, was written even as he took shelter in a bomb crater from a two-way bombardment that had caught him on open ground. The war, however, led to one of the seminal experiences of his life. Being badly injured in the head and lying unconscious on an operating table, he experienced an "out of body" state that convinced him there is something in man that can exist independently of the body.

While convalescing, Bennett was invited to join a course in the Turkish language because the army needed intelligence officers in the Near East. Throwing himself wholeheartedly into the task, as was his nature, he eventually found himself, at an absurdly early age, in Constantinople holding a very sensitive position between the British and the Turks. Fluency in Turkish made him the confidant of many high-ranking political figures there, and it allowed him to develop the knowledge and love of Turkey that would remain with him all his life. More importantly, he began to understand other modes of thought than European.

In 1921, in the aftermath of the Great War and the Russian Revolution, Constantinople was the center of great ferment and change. It was also the funnel through which many displaced persons passed on their way to the West, and it was part of Bennett's job to monitor their movement. Among these "displaced persons" were two most extraordinary men, with whom "circumstance" brought Bennett into contact: G.I. Gurdjieff and P.D. Ouspensky.

Bennett met Gurdjieff through a close friend in the Turkish royal family, Prince Sabaheddin, a reformist thinker and a profoundly spiritual man. Bennett's intermittent meetings with Gurdjieff and Ouspensky in Constantinople shaped the direction of his later spiritual search. But when they moved on to Europe, Bennett remained in Turkey, fascinated by the labyrinthine political and social developments that finally led to the overthrow of the sultanate and to the establishment of the Turkish republic.

His immersion in Turkish affairs and his relationship with Winifred Beaumont, an English woman living in Turkey, completed the growing estrangement from his first wife, Evelyn, who had remained in England. Bennett had married young—too young, perhaps—immediately after the war, and despite the birth of a daughter, Ann, their marriage didn't last. After the divorce, Bennett married Mrs. Beaumont, a woman twenty years his senior, and they remained together until she died forty years later.

When Bennett returned to England, he was consulted by the government as an expert on the Middle East, and he acted as an interpreter at the London Conference in 1924, which was supposed to settle matters between Turkey and Greece. He could have then taken up a career in public life and was invited to stand for parliament, but it was already clear to Bennett that his spiritual search would take priority.

In the summer of 1923 he renewed his connection with Gurdjieff and spent three months at Gurdjieff's Institute in France. In spite of the shortness of his stay, Bennett was shown things that convinced him that man is capable of spiritual transformation and that Gurdjieff had profound knowledge and understanding of the techniques by which this could be achieved. Gurdjieff told Bennett that he could help him make significant progress if he would spend two years at the institute. With hindsight, it seems strange that Bennett nevertheless felt obliged to leave, but he was very short of money and felt he needed to put his affairs in order. In any case, he expected to return to Gurdjieff soon; however, they did not meet again until 1948.

Back in England, Bennett joined P.D. Ouspensky's groups studying the "system," which Ouspensky had learned from Gurdjieff. Bennett remained with Ouspensky for fifteen years, during which time his professional life took several bizarre turns. He was involved in various brown-coal mining ventures in Greece and Turkey, which, though ultimate failures, did nevertheless give him an expertise in mining and the chemistry of coal. He spent four years based in Greece and was involved in protracted machinations involving land claims of members of the deposed Turkish royal family. During this period, Bennett led something of a buccaneering existence, but by the mid-1930s, he was back in England and involved in the coal industry once again. In 1938, he was asked to head Britain's first industrial research organization, the British Coal Utilisation Research Association (BCURA).

BCURA grew in importance with the start of World War II, and research concentrated on finding a coal-based alternative to oil. BCURA developed coal-gas-powered cars, a coal-based plastic, and, more significant if mundane, efficient fireplaces that gave more heat for less fuel. All this time, Bennett continued to work with Ouspensky and the ideas and methods of the "system."

By 1941, when Ouspensky left England to live in the United States, Bennett was running his own study groups and giving his own lectures. Throughout the Second World War, and in spite of it, the groups continued and expanded in London while Bennett began writing and developing his own ideas as well as Gurdjieff's. But it was not until 1947, when he was fifty, that Bennett published his first book, *The Crisis in Human Affairs.*

People who came to hear his public lectures and those who joined his private groups found a tall, imposing figure, blue eyed and younger looking than his age. Essentially a shy man, not given to small talk, he possessed an intellect that some people found intimidating. When he began lecturing he was nervous, but very soon he abandoned the use of notes and thereafter always spoke spontaneously. As he grew older, his lectures became one of the principle ways in which he developed his ideas. He was literally "thinking on his feet." Several of his books had their beginnings as lecture transcripts, and the talks Bennett gave at Sherborne House in the few years before he died produced some extraordinary insights.

In 1946, Bennett bought Coombe Springs, a seven-acre estate a few miles southwest of London with several buildings and an Edwardian villa on it. He and his wife acquired the property with the intention of starting a small research community. They moved in with ten of his closest pupils, and for twenty years Coombe Springs became a center for group work, attracting hundreds of people.

All the while, publicly Bennett continued to expound Gurdjieff's ideas, but privately his inner life was in turmoil. Ouspensky had repudiated him in 1945, which proved very painful, and he had lost touch with Gurdjieff—whom he had long regarded as his teacher—believing him to be dead. So the discovery in 1948 that Gurdjieff was alive and living in Paris was highly significant. In the remaining eighteen months before Gurdjieff died (on October 29, 1949) Bennett took every opportunity to go to Paris—usually during the weekend—despite his heavy professional schedule (at Powell Duffryn, the coal company for whom he now worked) and his responsibility for group work at Coombe Springs.

In the summer of 1949, he spent a month working very intensively with Gurdjieff in Paris, and this experience laid the foundation for a significant transformation in his life and spiritual work. It was a turning point, and in the remaining twenty-five years of his life Bennett became more approachable and more compassionate. Considering how little actual time he spent with Gurdjieff, it is extraordinary how much he made of the opportunities.

Gurdjieff's death was a serious blow for Bennett, as it was for all of Gurdjieff's followers. For a while they were able to work together, but gradually factions appeared—partly derived from Gurdjieff's own tendency to sow confusion by giving conflicting authority to his closest associates. In Bennett's case, the conflict was exacerbated by his own willingness to take Gurdjieff's ideas and develop them further and, as he put it in the introduction to his book on Gurdjieff,* to struggle to "make something of them for himself."

*Gurdjieff: Making a New World (New York: Harper and Row, 1976).

In 1950 Bennett gave up his professional life, subsequently resisting several attractive offers to return to a career in industrial administration and research, and concentrated instead on the group work at Coombe Springs. He lectured frequently about Gurdjieff's system, trying to fulfill a promise he had made to Gurdjieff to do all in his power to spread the ideas and make them understood. In 1953, he undertook a long journey to the Middle East, which brought him into personal contact with the religion of Islam and various Sufi orders. * When he returned to England, he initiated a project to build a large meeting hall at Coombe Springs. The unusual nine-sided architectural design was based on the enneagram, an ancient symbol presented by Gurdjieff as embodying the fundamental laws of nature. The building took two years to complete, and at the opening in 1957, Bennett commented that the real value of such a project was in building a community rather than the building itself. And there certainly was a great deal of energy at Coombe Springs at the time.

Then, later in 1957, Bennett shook the whole place up with his involvement in Subud, a spiritual movement that had newly appeared from Indonesia. For a number of reasons, Bennett felt that Gurdjieff had expected the arrival of a teaching from that country, and, having tried the Subud spiritual exercise himself, he threw himself with characteristic energy into helping Pak Subuh, the movement's founder, disperse his teaching. He traveled extensively to spread the Subud message, both with Pak Subuh and on his own. He learned Indonesian and was so able to translate Pak Subuh's lectures into various languages. Bennett's own introductory book, *Concerning Subud,* sold thousands of copies worldwide.

Some of Bennett's pupils were dismayed, and his enthusiasm for Subud deepened the divisions with some of the other Gurdjieff groups in London and Paris. Subud—with its emphasis on submission to the will of God and its reliance on a single practice, the *latihan*—seemed to some to be the antithesis of Gurdjieff's methods for spiritual awakening, and many people left the Coombe Springs groups. Others, however, came in large numbers, and for several years Coombe Springs was the headquarters of the Subud movement in Europe. It attracted serious seekers *and* sensation seekers as well as unsolicited newspaper headlines. But by 1962, after devoting himself selflessly to

* *Journeys to Islamic Countries,* vols. 1–2 (England: Coombe Springs Press, 1977).

its growth and expansion, Bennett left the Subud organization, feeling that a return to the Gurdjieff method was necessary.

So, with a small group, Bennett began to work once again with Gurdjieff's system. He resumed work on the final volumes of his magnum opus, *The Dramatic Universe* (the first volume had been published in 1956; the second appeared in 1961), and in early 1963, he presented a plan to the council of the Institute for Comparative Study of History, Philosophy, and the Sciences—which actually owned Coombe Springs and which Bennett had founded in 1946—proposing a renewal of the community, which while still open to Subud members would be primarily one where people would be dedicated to spiritual transformation along the lines of the Gurdjieff system. Although he maintained to the end of his life that he had derived great benefit from Subud, it was now the turn of Subud members to be dismayed, and many turned against him.

Meanwhile, Bennett had made an important contact with a Hindu saint living in Nepal: the Shivapuri Baba, who was 135 years old when Bennett visited him in 1961. He went again in 1963, and once more he undertook to make known the ideas of another.* The simplicity and the rigor of the Shivapuri Baba's teaching appealed to Bennett, who was later to refer to the old saint as his teacher.

But by the mid–'60s, although the work at Coombe Springs had gathered new momentum, Bennett was ready to make yet another change. He and his groups had become involved with Idries Shah (who is now very well known as an exponent of Sufism but who was then just establishing himself in England), and once again Bennett offered his help. Along with the Institute for Comparative Study, he proposed giving the whole property of Coombe Springs over to Shah. It seemed a ridiculous notion, for the land was becoming very valuable, but, nevertheless, in the spring of 1966 the gift was made. But after Bennett and some of the Coombe Springs residents had moved into a house in the neighboring town of Kingston-upon-Thames, Shah, subsequently and in short order, sold Coombe Springs for a housing development!

Many thought Bennett had made another big mistake. But, in truth, Shah had performed a real service—quite the opposite of the way it appeared—by helping Bennett to become completely free of a place to which he had devoted twenty years of his life. Without that sacrifice, it is doubtful whether Bennett would have been able to embark on the

*J.G. Bennett, *Long Pilgrimage: The life and teaching of Sri Govindananda Bharati, known as the Shivapuri Baba* (San Francisco: Dawn Horse Press, 1983).

last and perhaps most significant project of his life: the inauguration of an experimental Fourth Way school for the passing on of techniques for spiritual transformation.

However, this school didn't happen immediately. For the next four years, Bennett lived quietly with his family: he had married Elizabeth Howard in 1958 following the death of his second wife and now had two sons and two young daughters. With a small group of scientists, he was developing "Systematics," a practical analytical method based on his own researches—and ultimately on what he had learned from Gurdjieff—into the laws governing processes in the natural world. This research led to an ill-fated attempt to market a structured learning method, but it is clear, with hindsight, that Bennett was waiting to see what his next task should be. All the while, he continued group work with his pupils and made new contacts with teachers in the Near East.

Then, in 1969, after becoming very dangerously ill and nearly dying (this experience is described in the last edition of his autobiography), he took another important step in his spiritual life, one that appeared to change him fundamentally. Shortly after this bout with death, he became very interested in the condition of young people, especially those who surfaced following the social and cultural turmoil of the '60s with serious questions about the significance of life but with few satisfactory answers. As part of his research into the way they were feeling, Bennett even attended the huge rock music festival on the Isle of Wight (off the southern coast of England) in 1970. The outcome of all this was the setting up of an "academy" to teach some of what he had learned during a lifetime of trying to discover the "sense and aim of life, and of human life in particular."

Initially, he thought in terms of two dozen students working in Kingston, but he soon realized that work on the land—an essential part of any program to teach people about the proper relationship between mankind and the rest of creation—would require a larger number. And then there was the unforeseen huge response to his proposal—particularly in the United States. So very quickly he attracted one hundred pupils, and in the fall of 1971, with the support of the Institute for Comparative Study, he inaugurated "Sherborne," the International Academy for Continuous Education, in the village of Sherborne, Gloucestershire, England.

The ten-month courses, of which he proposed five "as an experiment," proved fruitful, and many people have continued, as he had hoped, to work with the ideas and methods he presented. His aim was to run the courses and then—in characteristic fashion—to do something else. However, he died shortly after the start of the fourth course, on December 13, 1974. That course and the fifth were completed by his wife, Elizabeth, working with a few of his most experienced pupils.

What he would have done had he lived another decade is a matter of conjecture. In the months before he died, Bennett worked hard to establish an experimental "ideal human society" embodying the methods and ideas that he had developed and derived from Gurdjieff. He made big efforts to overcome the rifts that had grown between different groups of Gurdjieff's followers, and what is most intriguing, he was beginning to talk about the development of new forms of worship* appropriate for the modern world.

J.G. Bennett left a legacy of selfless giving and unrelenting inquiry into the mystery and meaning of existence. He published numerous works (many unfortunately now out of print), inspired hundreds to seek reality at the expense of self-centeredness, and stimulated the formation of groups of students who have continued to work with the ideas and methods he passed on at Sherborne and Coombe Springs. These people are continuing to this day to learn from his example: that if one wants to follow a system of ideas of spiritual transformation, one has to work with them and try to make something of them for oneself.

—George Bennett
Cave Junction, Oregon
October 1989

---

* J.G. Bennett, *Sacred Influences* (Santa Fe: Bennett Books, 1989).

Publisher's Notes

All quotations are by J.G. Bennett unless otherwise referenced.
For bibliographic details on his books, see Bibliography.

Notes to Pages 7–20

Chapter 1, The World Situation

1. The talks from which this chapter was compiled were given to students at the International Academy for Continuous Education in 1973. Some parts near the end of the chapter are from a public lecture given at Caxton Hall, London, in December of that same year.

2. "The third or reconciling principle is in [man's] emotional nature. . . . It is a Universal Spiritual Power as might be understood either from the Great Spirit doctrine, or from the Christian notion of the Holy Spirit as the Universal Love . . . whereby the Godhead is united with the Creation." From *Gurdjieff: Making a New World,* 248.

Needless to say, it is the condition of our "emotional" or feeling nature that is today the source of much suffering and confusion. Bennett, in the above referenced work and in several other books, gives many new insights into this feeling aspect of human nature and offers practical guidance, based on sacred tradition, as to how we can work with it.

3. The five "being-obligolnian-strivings" of Ashiata Shiemash are instruments by which real conscience can be awakened in us as we progress along our path of self-perfecting. The reader is referred to G.I. Gurdjieff, *Beelzebub's Tales to His Grandson* (New York: E.P. Dutton & Co., Inc., 1964), 386.

4. "There is a well-known view that associates the cycles of history with the precession of the equinoxes and divides the great year—or great cycle—of twenty-five thousand sidereal years into twelve signs of the zodiac. I have not been able to verify this and have noted that the most ancient records divide the sky into ten and not twelve regions. This gives the duration of two thousand five hundred years for each minor cycle or epoch, which fits historical evidence very much better." From *The Masters of Wisdom,* 42.

The reader is referred to chapter 2, "The Early Masters," of *The Masters of Wisdom,* in which Bennett traces the history of the ten thousand years before Christ, dividing that time into four epochs: the Epoch of Withdrawal and Concentration; the Epoch of Diffusion; the Epoch of Conflict; and the Heroic Epoch. *See also* chapter 4 of this book, "The Spirit of a Society."

5. This obligation is beautifully expressed in the prayer before meals that Mr. Bennett introduced to students at his experimental Fourth Way school, The International Academy for Continuous Education ("Sherborne"): "All life is one; and everything that lives is holy. Plants, animals, and men all must eat to live and nourish one another. We bless the lives that have died to give us this food. Let us eat consciously, resolving by our 'work' to pay the debt of our existence."

Quite a lot can be said about what it means to "eat consciously"; and there is much misunderstanding, confusion, and fantasy in our relationship to food. Being conscious of the first bite at mealtimes does, however, play an important part in the process of energy transformation begun with the taking of food. The reader is referred to P.D. Ouspensky, *In Search of the Miraculous* (New York: Harcourt, Brace & World, Inc.,1949), 181–192.

6. Cf. G.I. Gurdjieff, "Religion," in *All and Everything: An Objectively Impartial Criticism of the Life of Man, or Beelzebub's Tales to His Grandson* (New York: Harcourt, Brace & Company, 1950; E. P. Dutton & Co., Inc., 1964), 723–726.

7. This is why Bennett agreed to have the work at Sherborne filmed (for the BBC program "One Pair of Eyes"), whereas fifteen years before he would have nothing to do with such a project. [Note from original edition.]

8. "Gurdjieff asserts in *Beelzebub's Tales* that the doctrine of reciprocal maintenance is derived from 'an ancient Sumerian manuscript' discovered by the great Kurdish philosopher Atarnakh. The passage quoted runs: 'In all probability, there exists in the world some law of the reciprocal maintenance of everything existing. Obviously our lives serve also for maintaining something great or small in the world (*All and Everything*, chap. 43, p. 1094).'" From *Gurdjieff: Making a New World*, 189.

9. Inner spiritual exercises that are done in a mediation-like sitting position, some of which have to do with the awakening of energie, such as "self-remembering" and "non-indentifying," that are needed for "work on oneself."

10. "[Gurdjieff] shows that in the limitations imposed by the conditions of existence in the universe there is present a denying force. This force is not of itself evil; indeed it is necessary to enable the divine purpose to be made manifest." From *Gurdjieff: Making a New World*, 199.

Notes to Pages 23–37

Chapter 2, Spiritual Community

1. This and part 1 of chapter 6, "The Sermon on the Mount," both from 1968, are the only parts of this book not given during the years of the experimental International Academy for Continuous Education. Those interested in a deeper exploration of the cosmological ideas that Bennett presents briefly here are directed to his four-volume masterwork, *The Dramatic Universe*.

"*The Dramatic Universe* is a search for an adequate description of the whole of human experience, the unknowable as well as the knowable, the historical as well as the timeless, the domain of value as well as the domain of fact. Man can never be understood as a being existing just in this visible world. Even for material existence it is not enough to think in terms of one world. Reality is uncertain and no laws are absolute." From the précis to the first edition.

2. Eternity: the storehouse of potentialities; one of the four determining conditions together with space, time, and hyparxis. Eternity is the measure of intensity of being. (Reference: *The Dramatic Universe*, vol. 1, *The Foundations of Natural Philosophy*.)

3. Hyparxis: the condition of ableness to be; one of the four determining con-

ditions together with space, time, and eternity. (Reference: *The Dramatic Universe,* vol. 1.)

4. For a deeper understanding of what Bennett means by such terms as World of Realization and Hyparchic Future, the interested reader is referred to *The Dramatic Universe,* vol. 1.

5. Existence: the element of "being" (the togetherness of experience) in all existence. Existence is all possible being. (Reference: *The Dramatic Universe,* vol. 1.)

6. Bennett, in his book *Gurdjieff: Making a New World,* uses the term "Demiurgic Intelligence" to refer to "agencies that we cannot perceive with our senses or even know with our minds" but with whom we must cooperate because these higher or angelic powers are "responsible for the orderly [evolutionary] progress of the solar system." The reader is referred to J.G. Bennett, "The Demiurge," chap. 1 in *The Masters of Wisdom.*

Notes to Pages 39–42

Chapter 3. The Three Orders of Society

1. This chapter is from a talk to students at Sherborne House in 1973. "The way foreordained by our Endless Creator for the perfection of three-brained beings is 'conscious labors and intentional sufferings [being-parktdolg duty].' This belongs to the spiritual reality and we cannot think about it in any ordinary way." From *Talks on Beelzebub's Tales,* 123.

2. This is a reference to G.I. Gurdjieff, "The Organization for Man's Existence Created by the Very Saintly Ashiata Shiemash," chap. 28 in *All and Everything: Beelzebub's Tales to His Grandson.*

3. "Reciprocal maintenance in its special sense connotes that the universe has a built-in structure or pattern whereby every class of existing things produces energies or substances that are required for maintaining the existence of other classes." From *Gurdjieff: Making a New World,* 189. *See also* chap. 1, note 8.

4. *See* this chapter's note 2.

Notes to Pages 43–49

Chapter 4, The Spirit of Society

1. This chapter is from a talk to students at Sherborne House in 1973. The term "spirit" refers to the spirit world, the *alam-i arvah,* where existence does not take the form of extension in space and duration in time. This is the world of dreams, of mind, of the finer energies, which is not just mind but a complete world with its own laws and ecology. [Note from original edition.]

2. Cf. Bennett's notion of a fifth dimension, "eternity." *The Dramatic Universe,* pass. [Note from original edition.]

3. The reader is referred to *The Masters of Wisdom,* chap. 1, 2.

4. God dies to help man. Shiva drinks the world poison, Mitra is sacrificed to save the world. There are far more ancient examples. [Note from original edition.]

Notes to Pages 51-55

Chapter 5, Psychokinetic Communities

1. This chapter is from a talk to students at Sherborne House in 1974. The Khwajagan were, in Bennett's terminology, "masters of wisdom" who differed "from 'experts in manipulation' by their ability to see the reality of the situation, by their freedom from egoism, and by their ability to cooperate with one another. . . . They are in contact with the higher wisdom that surveys life on this earth as a whole and can see whence it has come and whither it is destined to go." From *The Masters of Wisdom,* 22.

2. G.I. Gurdjieff, "The Chief Culprit in the Destruction of All the Saintly Labors of Ashiata Shiemash," chap. 28 in *Beelzebub's Tales to His Grandson.*

3. The Bektashis are spiritual descendants of Hadji Bektash, a contemporary of Rumi, who settled in central Turkey in the thirteenth century.

Notes to Pages 57–71

Chapter 6. The Sermon on the Mount

1. Part 1 of this chapter is from a talk given in 1968. Part 2 was given to students at Sherborne House in 1973.

2. Cf. Dean Farrar: "Conceited illuminism is as deep an offence against charity as saintly self-satisfaction." [Note from original edition.]

3. This is a phonetic version. Pronounce as for English spelling. Mr. Bennett's facility with languages, and here in particular with Greek, allowed him to penetrate the mystery and significance of the Beatitudes.

4. "Chief feature" is one's individual characteristic that denies or blocks out the whole. The reference is to group meetings not recorded. [Note from original edition.] Cf. P.D. Ouspensky, *In Search of the Miraculous (New York: Harcourt, Brace & World, Inc., 1949),* 266–268.

Notes to Pages 72–73

Chapter 7, Characteristics of the Psychokinetic Life

1. This chapter is from a talk to students at Sherborne House in 1974. About the denying force: *see* chap. 1, note 10.

2. "What is this catastrophic event? There has come about a fundamental misconception of the significance of human life. Something goes wrong for people before they reach responsible age. Gurdjieff is not talking about egoism but about something that we do to our children." From "Cataclysm Not According to Law," in *Talks on Beelzebub's Tales.*

3. G.I. Gurdjieff, *All and Everything or Beelzebub's Tales to His Grandson* (New York: E.P. Dutton & Co., Inc., 1964), 1164. The phrase is written by God over the entrance to Purgatory. [Note from original edition.]

Bibliography of J.G. Bennett

Concerning Subud. London: Hodder and Stoughton, 1960.

The Crisis in Human Affairs. London: Hodder and Stoughton, 1954.

Creative Thinking. Charles Town, West Virginia: Claymont Communications, 1989.

Deeper Man. London: Turnstone Books, 1985.

The Dramatic Universe. vol. 1, The Foundations of Natural Philosophy. Abridged by Eric Mandel. Charles Town: Claymont Communications, 1987.

The Dramatic Universe. vol. 2, The Foundations of Moral Philosophy. Charles Town: Claymont Communications, 1987.

The Dramatic Universe. vol. 3, Man and His Nature. Charles Town: Claymont Communications, 1987.

The Dramatic Universe. vol. 4, History. Charles Town: Claymont Communications, 1987.

Enneagram Studies. York Beach, Maine: Weiser, 1983.

Energies—Material, Vital, Cosmic. Charles Town: Claymont Communications, 1989.

Gurdjieff: A Very Great Enigma. York Beach: Weiser, 1983.

Gurdjieff: Making a New World. New York: Harper and Row, 1976.

How We Do Things. Charles Town: Claymont Communications, 1989.

Hazard. Sherborne, England: Coombe Springs Press, 1976.

Idiots in Paris (with E. Bennett). England: Coombe Springs Press, 1980.

Intimations: Talks with J. G. Bennett at Beshara. New York: Weiser, 1975.

Journeys to Islamic Countries. vols. 1 & 2. Sherborne: Coombe Springs Press, 1977.

Long Pilgrimage: The Life and Teaching of Sri Govindananda Bharati, Known as the Shivapuri Baba. California: Dawn Horse Press, 1983.

Masters of Wisdom. London: Turnstone Press, 1980.

Needs of a New Age Community: Talks on Spiritual Community and Fourth Way Schools. Santa Fe: Bennett Books, 1990.

Sacred Influences: Spiritual Action in Human Life. Santa Fe: Bennett Books, 1989.

Sevenfold Work. Charles Town: Claymont Communications, 1979.

Sex. York Beach: Weiser, 1989.

A Spiritual Psychology. Lakemont, Georgia: CSA Press, 1974.

The Spiritual Hunger of the Modern Child (with others). Charles Town: Claymont Communications, 1984.

Sufi Spiritual Techniques. Ellingstring, England: Coombe Springs Press, 1982.

Talks on Beelzebub's Tales. York Beach: Weiser, 1988.

Transformation. Charles Town: Claymont Communications, 1978.

The Way to Be Free. New York: Weiser, 1980.

What Are We Living For? Sherborne: Coombe Springs Press, 1973.

Witness: The Autobiography of John G. Bennett. Charles Town: Claymont Communications, 1983.

✧